A Christian in the New Age

A Christian in the New Age

PETER SPINK

Foreword by Mary Edward House OP

Darton, Longman and Todd
London

First published in 1991 by
Darton, Longman and Todd Ltd
89 Lillie Road, London SW6 1UD

British Library Cataloguing in Publication Data
Spink, Peter
A Christian in the New Age
1. Christianity. Religious life
I. Title
248.4

ISBN 0–232–51897–1

Phototypeset by Input Typesetting Ltd, London SW19 8DR
Printed and bound in Great Britain by
Courier International Ltd, Tiptree, Essex

To Pamela
who first said 'write'

Contents

Foreword

Christians over the ages have followed their pilgrimage of prayer, have sought the hidden treasure, the pearl of great price. We learn by experience, and sometimes can find through others' shared experience, which paths to follow. Sometimes an unknown light shines on the way, and the familiar is transformed. Poets such as Herbert and Vaughan find the words to share their glimpses of eternity. In our own day the priest-poet R.S. Thomas tells of his own journey and of his realization that prayer can be

> . . . the annihilation of difference,
> the consciousness of myself in you,
> of you in me . . .

In the New Age of heightened awareness many are engaged on the spiritual quest. In this age barriers are falling. The destruction of the Berlin Wall is not only a literal reality but a powerful symbol of the transcendence of old divisions, and of the power of the dynamic over the static. Teilhard de Chardin, who spoke originally to a hostile audience unready to accept him, has become accessible to many minds and kindled hope in many hearts. Above all, Christ 'who has made both one' offers the way, the truth and the life to all who can see the Glory of God shining in his face.

For the Christian in the New Age, Peter Spink is a wise guide. His is the voice of authentic experience, the voice of a healer and a contemplative.

This book will point its readers to the God within, and help us to enter our inheritance.

MARY EDWARD HOUSE OP
Prioress General
English Dominican Sisters of St Catherine of Siena

Introduction

'Haven't you heard about the New Age?' The questioner was one of a group of young people taking part in a conference on the island of Iona. The conference theme was 'Spiritual Awakening in our Day' and I had been sent by my bishop to investigate.

The week-long event had been organized by the Wrekin Trust, which describes itself as an 'educational charity concerned with promoting awareness and study of the spiritual principles that operate through us and in the universe'. In reply to my questioner, I confessed that in this year of our Lord 1972 I was entirely ignorant of this alleged new epoch, and asked to be enlightened.

During the next few days, between lectures and seminars, I was presented with a package deal, the contents of which appeared to embrace mysticism, various esoteric traditions, healing, astrology and much else besides. The whole was bound together by apocalyptic expectations of tremendous changes, both within the human psyche and in society at large. I was puzzled yet at the same time fascinated. Here was what at first sight appeared to be a group of way-out, ungrounded visionaries dabbling in 'isms' old and new, and all of this was quite divorced from the realities of life as I perceived them to be. Yet I became increasingly aware, as the conference ran its course, that there was much more to what I had judged to be these hippy non-conformists than either their dress or vocabulary would appear to indicate.

The convenor and chairman of the conference was Sir George Trevelyan. A powerful, charismatic speaker, coming from a distinguished establishment family, Sir George had grown up against a background of Liberal politics and progressive thought. His great-grandfather had been head of the Treasury and his grandfather in Gladstone's Liberal cabinet. His uncle was the well-known historian. He himself had read history at Cambridge and later taught at Gordonstoun. As Principal of Attingham Park Adult College he began his pioneering work in 'the communicating of spiritual knowledge'. Clearly much of his inspiration was derived from the teaching of Rudolf Steiner's concept of the Cosmic Christ, but his vision of human potential and destiny could not be confined to any one set of spiritual disciplines. When asked about his religious affiliation, Sir George would reply disarmingly and with great charm, 'Oh, Church of England!' In 1971 he founded the Wrekin Trust which now has an outreach not only in the British Isles but throughout the English-speaking world.

Amongst the extraordinary speakers at the conference, who ranged from a scientist to a lay healer, none was more impressive than a Polish Roman Catholic priest who was also a scientist. His addresses were for me 'mind-blowing', in that they gave a significance in evolutionary terms to Christ's death and resurrection which my own theological training had not remotely conceived. When I first saw Fr Andrew Glazewski, affectionately known as 'glass-whisky', he was celebrating Mass in the centre of the hotel lounge. He wore no vestments and his altar was a coffee table. Surrounding him, and mostly sitting on the floor, was a crowd of young people, all apparently completely at one with the mystery of the Mass. It was as though the ritual had surrendered itself to the reality. 'Here is a totally New Age priest,' whispered someone at my elbow, 'a man before his time.' 'Look at his aura,' said another. I looked and could see nothing, but I was aware of a real 'presence' that filled the room.

Not long after this, and whilst taking part in a similar conference, this remarkable man died. His influence in fostering the truly spiritual impulses inherent within the New Age phenomena is incalculable and is still, at the beginning of the 1990s, widely felt.

For me the whole Iona event constituted a disconcerting paradox. Most of the participants spoke a language that I simply did not understand. Spiritual issues were expounded and discussed in what appeared to me to be esoteric and psychological terms rather than those of theology. Nevertheless, seven days of sharing with the hundred or so participants required me to recognize a spiritual integrity and a deep sense of what I felt sure St Paul would have described as '*agape*'. I was also beginning to understand that truth can never be equated with the particular thought-forms in which it is clothed and by which it is expressed.

I left the island pondering hard the need for discernment, for I had become acutely conscious that beneath what appeared to be a mass of conflicting belief patterns there was a bedrock of shared spiritual experience and perception, authenticated by the fruits of the Spirit.

It would have been easy to dismiss the whole as a revival of the ancient heresy known as Gnosticism; but such a judgement would not square with all that I had seen and experienced, and I determined at least to keep in mind the warm invitation I had received from the young people to 'Come and visit our Centre.' A journey had begun for me, and I knew I could not turn back.

I have often reflected on my bishop's words when he suggested that I attend the conference: 'It all sounds rather different, and you never know what may come out of it.' Certainly there came out of it for me what I can only describe as a powerful precipitation into a long search involving many new experiences. These were to lead to a fresh comprehension, both of Christian ministry and of what Teilhard de Chardin called the 'splendour of Christ's glorious countenance'.

It was also to mean for me the realization of a splendid

paradox, for I began to see the Church as the privileged custodian of tremendous truths, the full significance of which it rarely fully perceives.

Eventually I was to discover that there were more aspects to what I was now beginning to describe as the 'new consciousness'. Some of these were far less grounded in reality than what had been expressed through the lives of the young people who first questioned me. Yet all this was part of a phenomenon that I was determined, as the bishop had originally commissioned me to do, 'to investigate'. What very soon became abundantly clear to me was that if we are to begin to understand the nature and significance of all that is happening, it is first of all important to distinguish between peripheral phenomena on the one hand and the authentic essence on the other. The former constitutes endless wanderings in the labyrinthine ways of psychic culs-de-sac, the latter touches a powerful creative dynamic which is even now giving birth to new patterns of growth in society. It is with these new impulses that this book is primarily concerned.

1

The New Age Phenomenon

Where and how did all this begin?

In the later 1950s Western civilization entered a period of change and transformation, the speed of which is perhaps unparalleled in any previous stage of recorded history. Almost everything that had been accepted by earlier generations as essential to the stability and good order of society came to be questioned, and in many instances rejected, by the younger generation. A process of ruthless demolition of what were seen as hypocritical conventions and outmoded standards began, and continued over a period of more than twenty years.

At the heart of this revolution in consciousness was a desire on the part of many to break free from the paternalistic shackles imposed by traditional institutions, whether secular or religious. For these, it was felt, prevented the development of personal responsibility and growth into maturity. In what this revolution itself would soon regard as sexist language, a religious leader of the day, Bishop John Robinson, declared that man had come of age and was determined to take control of his own destiny.

A significant factor in what an older generation saw as a headlong plunge toward chaos and anarchy was a widespread disillusionment with Western science and technology. What had been regarded as great human achievements were beginning to turn in upon themselves, and that which until now had been hailed as progress was seen to contain all the seeds of self-destruction.

Nuclear power, far from being the answer to an increasing need for new sources of energy which its advocates had promised, seemed to spell nothing but contamination, both for the human race and for the planet. The pollution of the earth and the near-disastrous consequences to all living things, appeared as an overwhelming spectre obliterating all hope for the future. Western ideas of progress and Western materialistic values were rejected on every hand.

In the face of this collapse of confidence in inherited values and institutions, signs began to appear of the beginnings of a search for doors into the interior, and what many hoped would prove to be spiritual, world. A new security was being sought; the journey inward, the quest for heart wisdom, had begun.

Confronted with this entirely new and startling search for an inner life, the established Churches appeared helpless and unprepared. 'Contemplation', which was what this was apparently all about, had always been according to the Western Christian tradition the prerogative of an élitist and often suspect body known as 'mystics'. Furthermore, what was being sought seemed suspiciously akin to that practised by Eastern religions. Very quickly, with rare exceptions, the Churches became first of all defensive and then judgemental. Amongst the clergy there were clear echoes of Bishop Butler's comment upon the teachings of John Wesley: 'This is a horrid thing, a very horrid thing indeed.'

In the face of this rejection it was to the East that the new generation of seekers quickly turned. As if by a magnet thousands were drawn to India in their search for spiritual teachers and gurus. The great trek to the East had begun. Soon a two-way traffic was in operation, for gurus or 'spiritual masters' began to arrive in the United Kingdom and America, and quickly found a fertile soil for their teachings.

Everywhere in the United Kingdom there appeared outward and visible signs of what was happening. The orange robes of the disciples of Rajneesh and the shaved heads of the followers of Krishna Consciousness became common sights on the streets of our cities. The clash of cymbals and chants of 'Hari Krishna, Hari Ram', provided a startling alternative in the heart of London to the once equally strange but now highly respected Salvation Army band. Posters on the London Underground and advertisements in magazines proclaimed Schools of Meditation, offering enlightenment through the teachings of highly acclaimed gurus.

All this was by no means confined to the towns and cities for, if not commonplace, it was certainly not unusual to meet mendicant Buddhist monks with their begging bowls wandering through the lanes of rural Surrey. Not only the unchurched young were caught up in this type of experimentation and enquiry. Religious professionals within the Churches were also affected. Among the younger clergy were those who felt a strong rapport with the new seekers. They were also aware of their own lack of training in any real spiritual disciplines.

I remember meeting one such rebel while visiting a Buddhist monastery in Sussex. I had been told by a friend with whom I was staying that she had some new neighbours who 'came from somewhere in the East'. They appeared to be a community and were, as she put it, 'very friendly if rather odd'. I decided to call on them and was warmly received by the abbot, who invited me to join the community for their evening meditation. With some difficulty I found sitting space on the floor of what had once been the drawing room of this eighteenth-century house. A young Westerner recognizable as a monk by his brown robe and shaved head moved along to give me space. 'Who are you?' he enquired politely. 'An Anglican priest,' I replied. 'So am I,' he said with a grin. 'I am here for a year or two learning how to say my prayers.'

Parallel to this turning inward was the growing public concern with what one section of society saw as the climate of corrupting permissiveness and another as creative freedom. Everywhere moral issues were being examined. Almost all related to the generating, nurturing or terminating of human life: birth control, abortion, drugs, sexuality, euthanasia and, for all its many achievements, the inadequacies of certain aspects of modern orthodox medicine. Behind the debate, rarely explicit or recognized yet implicit in almost every statement made, lay the question posed by the Psalmist: 'What is man?' The conditioned reaction of the Church was to respond to the question with theological statements about God which, however true or sincerely presented, were for many, in the face of their search and deeply felt need, pieces of irrelevant information.

The starting point of this new enquiry was not God but the human being. There appeared to be considerable justification for the common accusation that the clergy are past masters at the art of answering questions that nobody is asking! Again, the answers were to come from the East and from esoteric schools rooted in Eastern philosophies. Books on anthroposophy, a system formulated by Rudolf Steiner at the beginning of the century, with its 'maps of consciousness' and 'knowledge of Higher Worlds', began to appear, not only on the popular bookstalls but in the serious bookshops. A new picture of the human being in all its alleged totality had arrived in the West, and everywhere there were avid students. The 'subtle anatomy' of man was now a subject for serious study, for all those seeking self-knowledge.

What was this new understanding?

According to many Eastern philosophies, the human being possesses not only a physical body but other vehicles by which its total being is expressed. These include emotional, mental and other bodies, variously described by different schools of thought. Such bodies are understood to possess '*chakras*', centres capable of receiving, transforming and transmitting energy. The main *chakras*, of which it is said there are seven, are thought to relate to the endocrine system, and through this to the physical body.

The theory of the subtle anatomy cannot be scientifically verified but, allowing for variety of definition, is uniformly substantiated by those claiming to have a particular kind of sensitivity. Growth into spiritual maturity is achieved by the activating of the 'higher *chakras*', chiefly that relating to the heart or 'pivotal' centre. This is sometimes referred to as the 'Christ centre', which is activated as we become 'rooted and grounded in love'.

Other books with a special appeal began to appear. These offered interpretations and rationales of what was happening. The astrologically inclined described it as the passing from the Age of Pisces to the Age of Aquarius . . . hence a 'New Age'. The birth pangs which brought forth this child of Aquarius were in large part a rejection of the establishment institutions of the day. External authority, dogmatism and its corollary, blind faith, with the structures erected for their enforcement, were perceived as inimical to the new age of Aquarius.

The precious and loudly-acclaimed being which had been brought to birth was to be nourished and fed by the Ancient Wisdom, hidden during the Piscean Age from all but the few, but now freely available. At the heart of this wisdom was knowledge, a knowledge of the human being's true multi-dimensional constitution and its divine destiny. Faith, in the words of the hymn, was now to 'vanish into sight'. For those familiar with the imagery of the Book of Revelation, the New Jerusalem was 'coming down out of heaven'.

The great 'power' centres of Glastonbury and Stonehenge assumed for many a new significance. Pilgrimages to these and other 'centres of power', with the purpose of 'activating and relating to the energies', came into vogue. An assortment of esoteric schools concerned with the mystical traditions of all the great religions began to speak openly of a 'New Age now breaking upon us'. The age of belief was to give way to an age of knowledge. Foremost amongst these was the Arcane School founded as long ago as 1923 by a woman of great spiritual stature, Alice Bailey. One of the School's basic tenets was that a new and spiritually mature type of human being (mature in terms of potential) would begin to emerge from the middle of this century. Although operating from within a very different theological framework, Alice Bailey's perceptions of God are remarkably like those of the German theologian Paul Tillich, popularized by Bishop John Robinson in his book *Honest to God*, describing God as the 'Ground of our being'. Like all similar esoteric societies, the Arcane School gives great importance to the practice of meditation and those spiritual disciplines which belong to the mystical path.

Evolutionists, reinforced particularly by the Jesuit priest-scientist Teilhard de Chardin in the West, and the Hindu philosopher Shri Aurobindo in the East, discerned in the great changes a leap in human consciousness and a growing awareness of the Cosmic Christ operating beyond the ecclesiastical boundaries.

Influential interpretations came also from the pen of a Congregational layman, C.F. Happold. In his book *Religious Faith and Twentieth Century Man* he anticipated a great change which he interpreted as follows:

> Something is happening in the world around us . . . May it not be that we are on the verge of one of those spiritual and mental leaps which have happened before in the history of mankind, eras when the corporate mentality and spirituality of man shift and new vistas and interpretations of the universe open up?

Happold then goes on to put forth the proposition that for the 'new man' now appearing 'the only acceptable religion will be a mystical one', mystical in the terms of 'experiential wisdom'.

In 1974, Colin Wilson wrote a preface to the book *A Geography of Consciousness* by William Arkle in which he refers to the 'present evolution and revolution'. 'There is', he says, 'a feeling that a new type of man has been emerging in the past two hundred years and that the human race is now ready for an evolutionary leap.'

Another writer who exercised considerable influence was J.G. Bennett. In *The Dramatic Universe*, a massive work in five volumes, Bennett in a chapter entitled 'The Next Age of Mind' wrote: 'During the past epoch man has developed and exploited his intellectual powers. A tendency so far scarcely perceptible is towards the awakening of new powers. These will be emotional and intuitive rather than intellectual and analytical.'

It was largely in response to these and similar writers that there sprang up all over the United Kingdom what became known as 'Open Centres'. These form no common organization, for each is independent and autonomous. Their common bond is to develop and share New Age understanding. They exist both in town and country, occupying large old country houses or tenement buildings in the suburbs. Some have a resident core group. Such residents exist to serve and share the common life with visitors and resident guests. Some constitute charitable trusts. Interests range from alternative medicine to ecological concern. The practice of meditation is common to all the centres, for this is seen as the path to spiritual awakening at the end of the twentieth century.

Probably the best known, and certainly the largest, of these centres is the now world-famous Findhorn Community in Scotland, to which thousands of young people come from many parts of the world to share in New Age experience and to study the philosophy behind it. Findhorn has since its foundation in the 1960s moved from a preoccupation with psychic phenomena to a very sophisticated educational programme, covering many disciplines from the arts to politics.

With the advent of the 1980s it became increasingly possible to distinguish between psychic phenomena and the spiritual reality. In 1983 I wrote as follows:

We are now moving towards the end of the first stage of New Age realization with its discovery of new dimensions and possibilities, its excitement and expectancy and the sometimes accompanying froth and bubble. Some of the harsh realities which have been happily alluded to in terms of apocalyptic generalities are now painfully emerging as economic, political and social pressures . . . On the one hand there will be those who continue to seek for novelty and excitement. This will prove to be a cul-de-sac of glamour and illusion. On the other there will be those who by treading the way of the cross will, as Jesus taught, 'find the true self'. (*The End of an Age*)

In the same year I was invited to speak at a 'One Earth' festival in New Zealand. Such festivals, taking place annually in different parts of the world, derive their inspiration from Findhorn. It was there that I was privileged to witness and share in some of the new and powerful emerging spiritual impulses.

The purpose of the festival was to demonstrate how a new consciousness is operating in many, apparently unrelated, disciplines. The team included a scientist, an agriculturalist, a psychiatrist, a business man, an economist, a musician, an artist and a healer. My brief was to speak on Christianity. Following the festival, workshops and seminars were held in all the main population centres in a great variety of venues, ranging from cathedrals to canteens. Everywhere there was widespread recognition of changes taking place within all the areas we represented, and at the same time a desire to understand some of the apparent anomalies and contradictions with which the New Age movement is beset. As I have already indicated, to do this it is necessary to make a clear distinction between the psychic and the spiritual.

The word 'psychic' requires some definition. It derives from the Greek word *psyche*, or 'soul'. In the Christian Scriptures it has a wide range of usage and embraces the whole non-physical dimension of the human being. In common parlance those are said to be psychic who have the power to make contact with dimensions beyond the reach of the five senses. Such people are sometimes said to have a sixth sense.

Spiritual perception and psychic awareness are fundamentally different. Psychic awareness is an instinctual activity and a residue from an earlier stage of human evolution. Spiritual perception may be described as intuitive knowledge which comes to birth with the awakening of the heart. The man or woman described as psychic has a spontaneous and sometimes uncontrollable cognition of the world of emotions as they emanate from people and places. A typical example of the operation of this faculty is when a psychic walking into a particular room picks up the emotions which have been or are in operation in that room. Instinct, operating from the emotional centre within the human being, penetrates and frequently links with the world of emotions, a world that is impermanent and ever-changing. Intuition, or spiritual perception, apprehends the reasons behind the emotions and sees without fear, judgement or reaction.

In the context of the upheavals we have been examining there has been a great proliferation of psychic activity, often spontaneous and frequently not understood. This psychic activity is not to be dismissed on the one hand as 'evil' nor on the other glamorized into a spiritual awakening. Psychic ability is in itself neither good nor bad, for it has no ethical content. It consists of power and in itself is entirely neutral. The current manifestations are the result of the great release of emotional energy which the removal of restraints has made possible. This we shall examine later.

Psychic energy must be judged by the use to which it is put. As power in the hands of egocentric people, whether religious or otherwise, it may become the means of an unhealthy control over others. This may be done even in the name of religion. But those only are susceptible who give such power place, space or cognizance.

It is this understanding which must be applied when testing the 'validity' or otherwise of the New Age phenomenon.

2

The Hidden Worlds

Opposite the Royal Albert Hall stands one of the most eloquent of London's nineteenth-century memorials. It commemorates the Consort of Queen Victoria, Prince Albert, patron of the arts and sciences, but its significance is greater than that of a tribute to one man. The memorial symbolizes the approaching climax of the great wave of energy which was released in the fifteenth century by the Renaissance. As the nineteenth century reached its conclusion man was approaching his zenith as a secular being, and the nation's supreme self-confidence at that time was expressed in a parody of Christian Scripture: 'Glory to man in the highest, for man is the master of things.'

Within a very few years the tide began to turn. The first quarter of the twentieth century was, in spite of the final burst of energy which ushered in the atomic age, the time of disillusionment. The theory of inevitable development (the corollary of Renaissance achievement) was shattered by the 1914–18 war.

It was this seedbed of disillusionment with humanity's capacity to control its own destiny that gave birth to new energies and to a dynamic that was to open up the interior world of the human being. That world, central to New Age consciousness, is the universe within. The period of history which exploded the myth of humanity's inevitable march of progress was to witness the rise of pioneers, seers and thinkers who would open up new dimensions in humanity's understanding of itself.

Two significant areas of this development can be traced. The first of these was that of psychological medicine, pioneered by Freud and Jung against the weight of established psychologically mechanistic views of human nature. Together these two postulated and presented to the world a revolutionary view of humanity and of the treatment of disease. The movement which was to establish a psychosomatic basis for many forms of ill health had begun. The effect of human emotions on the subconscious mind, the existence of which was now accepted, and their subsequent effect on physical and mental states, was recognized to be at least an area for legitimate investigation. The hidden world of the unconscious had been recognized and was opening up to scientific method. Although after more than half a century of study and investigation the full implications of this have yet to be realized in medical practice, its basic assumptions, that is the world of the subconscious and the power and significance of human emotions in this world, have found acceptance in the science of medicine.

The second of these movements developed with a twofold strand – that of theosophy, that is the study of the nature of God, and anthroposophy, the study of the nature of man. Both had existed from time immemorial in the East, but were largely unknown in the West except within the very exclusive circles of some occult societies. The initiator of the Western theosophical movement was an extraordinary woman born in the first quarter of the nineteenth century, a Russian, Madame Blavatsky. Her disciple, an equally remarkable woman, Annie Besant, established the Theosophical Society. It is of interest to note that Annie Besant combined her studies of the arcane with a thorough knowledge of and activity in the political world of her day. She saw the two as essentially related.

Anthroposophy as a system was developed and formulated by Rudolf Steiner, who related his esoteric studies to every field of human knowledge and endeavour. Such was his genius that on the basis of a vast amount of intuitively acquired knowledge he lectured with authority to doctors on medicine, farmers on agriculture, scientists on science and to the clergy on theology. He himself ascribed his phenomenal knowledge to an ability to read the 'Akashic Records'. These alleged records he described in his book *An Outline of Occult Science*:

> The facts concerning the primeval past have not passed beyond reach of occult research. If a being comes into corporeal existence his material part perishes after physical death, but the spiritual forces which from out of their own depth gave existence to the body do not disappear in this way. They leave their traces, their exact images behind them, impressed upon the spiritual groundwork of the world. Anyone who is able to raise his perceptive faculty through the visible to the invisible world attains at length a level on which he may see before him what may be compared to a vast spiritual panorama in which are recorded all the past events of the world history. These imperishable traces of everything immaterial are called in occult science 'The Akashic Records'.

Although the terms theosophy and anthroposophy suggest different areas of investigation, both were from the beginning essentially concerned with the multidimensional nature of man and with worlds beyond the physical to which he relates through non-physical dimensions of his being. According to this understanding, a conscious relationship is established with these worlds when man's normally sense-bound awareness is changed. To dismiss the founders of these two movements as esoteric obscurantists would be a mistake, for here were men and women of considerable intellectual stature, passionately concerned to bring to Renaissance man an awareness of these inner worlds, of the outer form of which he was already so splendidly aware.

Powerful systems of thought were thus established to disseminate in the West a knowledge of man and of the nature of his being which, it was believed, had flourished within the Christian Church until about the thirteenth century, and which had finally vanished with the rise of the Renaissance. They saw themselves as laying foundations against the day when Western man, fully incarnated into matter and fulfilled as a secular being, would seek again for this ancient wisdom and apply it to life on this planet. Thus a generally unnoticed few established a rationale of that which it was anticipated would one day enter into the experience of many, an anticipation which to those caught up in New Age movements appears now to be vindicated. It is one particular aspect of this rationale with which we are concerned, that is the 'objective' world of emotions and man's relationship to it.

According to the Ancient Wisdom to which we have referred, humans through a non-physical dimension of their being, both relate to and operate in an emotional world. This is described in New Age terminology as an 'astral world'. To this dimension of the human being the emotional world is as objectively real as is the terrestrial to the physical. Throughout their life span humans, by their behaviour patterns, relationships and the direction of their wills, are building up both the substance of their non-physical bodies and the world to which they relate.

It is important to remember that, although in describing these realities we are of necessity using the language of time and space, this astral world is understood to relate primarily to a fourth dimension, and only in a secondary sense to the spatial world of the physical. Nevertheless its significance for life on this planet is seen to be of paramount importance, for it is a world through which human behaviour, both collective and individual, is powerfully influenced. It is a world of power and powerful thought forms to which 'natural man', as he is described in the New Testament, is exposed, and by which he is shaped. Currents of energy from this world flow powerfully into the uncontrolled human psyche, determining the behaviour patterns of the human race to an extraordinary degree. It is also a world which is continuously being created and uncreated. This process is effected by the out-pouring of the totality of human emotions. The uncontrolled flow of negative forces creates a world of destructive power, a world vulnerable and susceptible only to the consciously-controlled forces of the highest of human emotions. To enlightened human beings is given the capacity not only to control, but to transmute, these emotions.

Into this world, consciousness is fully released at death. For with the dissolution of the physical body its subtle counterpart, inhabited by the essence or spirit, gravitates to that level in the world of emotions to which it is sympathetically linked, to the substance of which it contributes and of which it is an essential part. This world is in some sense a world of survival, although we should not equate survival with permanence, for the emotional body, like the physical, is subject to the laws of dissolution, described in the New Testament as the 'second death'. This astral world as understood by theosophy and anthroposophy is quite distinct from the world of pure spirit. It is not therefore the world of immortality. It is seen as potentially the world of transition into the spiritual, or world of spirit.

As we have seen, it is an inevitable consequence of today's search and probing into the nature of the human being that awareness of this world should be increased. This in turn prompts desire for further experience. Frequently this desire is expressed as enquiry into ways of raising consciousness. Because of the absence of clear guidelines this may lead to confusion and delusion; and where is guidance to be found?

This briefly has been the contribution of theosophy and anthroposophy to human self-knowledge during this century. The insights of both are now widely disseminated in Western society. Indeed they may be regarded as the very cornerstone of New Age philosophy. Their relevance to the contemporary situation is seen to be of great significance. This may be summed up as follows. Human beings are today caught up by forces beyond their control and to an extent never before experienced. At every level of society, and on a global scale, there is a rising consciousness, often coupled with deep fear, that the political, economic and social patterns of society are in the grip of a maelstrom of irreversible change. Forces beyond the understanding and control of even leaders of intellectual stature and integrity are determining a course toward destruction. Never before has the world of objective emotions impinged so powerfully upon human consciousness. Therefore now is the time for self-knowledge and the transforming of negative energies.

Nevertheless, in spite of the labours of pioneer thinkers in theosophy and anthroposophy, this unveiling of humanity's inner world and the means by which it may be understood has until now received no comparable recognition to that accorded to the movement which gave birth to psychiatry, nor has it gained any credibility with the systems it has sought to influence. Science and religion have remained aloof from its claims. Orthodox Western religious thought has consistently rejected the movement as being a form of gnosticism, and therefore outside the area of revealed truth; whilst Western science has dismissed its premises as beyond the category of verifiable truth. Nevertheless, although such knowledge and experience has for the scientific and religious establishment remained a closed book, the climate of spiritual enquiry in this country is now, three-quarters of a century after the initiation of the movement, being considerably influenced by theosophical and anthroposophical insights.

The reasons for this are not difficult to discover. On the one hand there is the widespread disenchantment with the results of the Western scientific method and the direction it has taken; and on the other, as we have seen, disillusionment with orthodox religion. Confidence in religious and scientific assertions which take no cognizance of the new realities is rapidly evaporating, and neither scientific nor religious dogmatism can quell the rising tide of enquiry. In the resulting vacuum it is anthroposophy and theosophy which appear to provide landmarks within the interior and non-physical worlds, and which offer guidance concerning the utilizing and transforming of these emotional forces. What has until now been an area of theory and speculation for metaphysical thinkers and sensitives, is rapidly appearing to many as relevant to the harsh realities of life in the latter days of the twentieth century. Anthroposophy and theosophy are seen to point towards the possibility of a leap forward into spiritual maturity, with human beings taking responsible control of their own destiny.

What are the various means by which understanding is being sought today? During my search I have observed the following categories: spontaneous change of consciousness in the case of those commonly called psychic, and of whom today there appear to be many, especially amongst the young; the use of drugs; the practice of particular meditative techniques; the conscious application of certain laws; and lastly these methods as parallels to the path of true spiritual development.

Let us examine these areas and methods. A spontaneous change of consciousness may occur in a sensitive person when exposed to a situation where psychic energy is generated. An example of this is that which not infrequently takes place in revivalist-type gatherings, whether New Age or religious. A build-up of intense emotional energy through repetitive singing precipitates participants into a sudden and acute awareness of the astral world with all its pressures. This is often confused with spiritual experience. It is however rare that in such a situation the reality of what is happening is recognized by those responsible for initiating the process. This is illustrated by the experience of a young woman known to me who attended a renewal meeting in a certain church where the emotional build-up was intense. Upon leaving the church she discovered, to her consternation and bewilderment, that she could see the auric field around a number of the people nearby. Returning to the church she sought an explanation from the leaders of the gathering. Totally misunderstanding the situation, they ascribed the phenomenon to 'the work of the devil'. She was then taken to one side and exorcized. Such examples are not infrequent today, both in renewal circles and New Age encounter groups. Because of lack of *gnosis*, it is rarely understood that consciousness has been changed by pressure of psychic/emotional forces.

The use of meditative techniques is a method commonly practised in psychic development circles. Meditation on the psychic centres of the subtle body is directed towards what is described as expansion of consciousness. This means is used by various spirituality groups, of which today there is a proliferation. When ethical criteria are applied to such development, and when the motivation is not self-centred, the level of perception may be high; but without such safeguards the breakthrough is frequently into the lower levels of the astral world where illusion and delusion abound. Instability and neurosis often accompany this kind of experimentation.

The use of drugs is a method involving violence to the psyche, to the brain and often to the body. At best it gives an awareness of the astral world and its forces divorced from any moral control. At worst it leads to disintegration of the whole personality.

The application of what anthroposophy describes as cosmic laws is done under the guidance of a teacher. For this method of development great dedication and singleness of aim are required. This path is described by Rudolf Steiner in his book already referred to, *Knowledge of Higher Worlds*. Very great emphasis is placed on purity of motive.

The last of the paths to which I have referred is that of a genuine spiritual development, that is, the use of techniques of prayer and meditation which centre in the heart and lead to realization of the true Self which, says Jesus Christ, a man will find only if he is prepared to allow the pseudo-self or ego to be put to death. It is from the point of such self-awareness that true perspectives of the astral world are formed, and where it is seen and understood in relation to good and evil, and to the evolution of the whole planet. The astral world is thus brought under the control of spirit and spiritual laws. To recognize that for numbers of people today the astral world has assumed

an objective reality does not require concurrence with all the
conclusions of anthroposophy and theosophy, nor acceptance
of the esoteric maps which they draw. It does nevertheless
underline the urgent need for true spiritual direction.

3

The Search for Identity

I have already indicated the difficulty encountered in understanding 'New Age' language. Particularly is this so when familiar words are given an apparently new meaning. A clear example of this is found in the phrase 'self-realization'. For those nurtured within the framework of a religion where the concept of the self is of that which is to be subdued, denied and put to death, this is at best a contradiction in terms and at worst rank heresy.

In my journey of enquiry I quickly discovered that this was not so, for the self to be realized was something quite other than that which according to St Paul must be crucified (Gal. 6.14). Nevertheless, for many a difficulty remains. For those whose religious and cultural background is that of orthodox Western Christianity, self-denial, not self-realization, indicates the pathway to spiritual awakening and growth. The thought patterns associated with the term and the psychology behind it appear alien. Here is the language of the East, not of the religion which for almost two thousand years has shaped the thinking and psychology of the West. However, for those who today form the spearhead of the great spiritual search beyond the ecclesiastical borders, this is their language. It underlies the new psychology basic to their understanding of human nature. A generation has emerged which has discarded the psychology which enshrined at its centre the concept of a guilty self and its corollary of a distant and wrathful Deity. New images of the human and the divine have appeared, and these images loom large in Western consciousness today.

Two factors have contributed to this development. The first of these may be described as the great disruption. In his book *Mrs 'Arris Goes To Paris*, Paul Gallico graphically describes the guilt complex of his central character. Mrs 'Arris belongs to the generation of post-churchgoing Christians. She represents those for whom the personal and corporate links with the ecclesiastical structure have largely disappeared. Yet this is not without a sense of guilt, for the occasional compulsive attendance at such special events as the Harvest Festival remain. Echoes of a vengeful Creator God still sound in the back of her mind. And this mind is still powerfully connected to the experience of her forebears. The psychic links still hold; they have yet to be broken. For Mrs 'Arris the image of a guilty self and a vengeful God persists. Self is synonymous with sin and God with judgement. Not so for the new generation. For the thought patterns formed over two thousand years are rapidly disappearing, not only from the conscious mind but from the collective subconscious of the race. The great disruption from the past is almost complete, and the ground, having been cleared, is now fertile for the new concept of the human and the divine.

The second significant factor is that of the influx of new thought patterns, ideas consonant with the philosophy and psychology basic to the religions of the East. Concepts of human selfhood found in Hinduism, Buddhism and the mystical traditions of Islam have taken root. For these are the sources from which the new consciousness is being fed.

Fundamental to all Hindu systems of spiritual development is the doctrine of the higher self; that dimension of the human being which, unlike the selves which constitute the personality and are part of the natural and illusory world, relate essentially to the invisible and the divine.

Buddhism as a religion recognizes no individual real selfhood but is based upon an understanding of a universal or cosmic self. Realization of this is achieved when the ignorance which chains the human being to the illusion of a separate individuality is dispelled. This happens with the development of a true knowledge, for it is knowledge that brings enlightenment and a realization of man's true identity.

In their concepts of human identity both Hinduism and Buddhism resonate with current Western thinking. Disillusionment with Western materialism has created the conditions for a ready acceptance of the Hindu philosophy of *maya* by which the material world is seen as an illusion, and the rejection of dogmatic belief systems has prepared the way for the more congenial agnosticism of Buddhism.

The religion of Islam comes into a separate category, for apart from its mystical tradition it has no comparable doctrine. Islamic mysticism is pervaded by an awareness of a self comparable to that of Buddhism and Hinduism. Here we find a self-realization which expresses itself as the 'I am'. This experience is exemplified in the life of the great Persian mystic, Hilaj, who in the tenth century, in an ecstasy of self-realization declared, 'I am God.' As a result he was put to death for blasphemy.

This in brief is the understanding which has penetrated into the thinking and feeling of Western humanity during the second half of the twentieth century, and this consciousness of self to be realized, an essence to be discovered or a potential to be awakened, is superseding the once dominant consciousness of a self to be denied. In short, preoccupation with guilt has given way to an awareness of possibility. The focus is no longer upon deficiency, but potential. Educational programmes basic to this search proliferate in the Open Centres. Two names figure prominently in this field, particularly in relationship to the new self-awareness: George Ivanovitch Gurdjieff and Roberto Assogioli. The influence of their teachings in forming psychological terms for the new self-consciousness is of considerable importance.

I first heard of Gurdjieff in conversation with a fellow Anglican priest, who I discovered to my great surprise was a trustee of the Gloucestershire Centre. 'Have you come across the great architect of the New Age self yet?' he enquired. Receiving the question literally, I replied that I had not yet met the gentleman in question. In a few sentences my friend sketched such an intriguing word-picture of George Ivanovitch Gurdjieff that I was immediately drawn to discover more. So central is Gurdjieff's teaching related to the new self-consciousness, that it is important to examine this in some detail.

Gurdjieff was born in 1890 in the Caucasus. From adolescence he was engaged in a restless search for an understanding of the inner self. He described it as 'an irrepressible stirring to understand the precise significance of the life process of all outward forms of breathing creatures and in particular of the aim of human life in the light of this interpretation'. To this end he devoted the whole of his extraordinary life. He travelled into the remote parts of Central Asia and led expeditions, suffering the most incredible privations and hardships, in Egypt, Crete, Sumaria, Assyria and Palestine. He visited monasteries and spiritual communities in regions stretching from Mount Athos to Ethiopia and the Sudan. In these regions he unearthed and investigated the Wisdom traditions of ancient civilizations. During his travels Gurdjieff subjected himself and those accompanying him to the most rigid ascetic practices. The declared aim of his search was to find the remnants or descendants of the living presence of human beings who were in contact with an undying core of true wisdom. Although his search carried him far beyond the boundaries of Christianity, he was baptized in the Russian Orthodox Church and was buried according to its rites in 1949.

In 1922 Gurdjieff settled near Fontainebleau in France, where he founded the Institute for the Harmonious Development of Man. Here he worked with students from all over Europe. Study, self-observation, physical work and sacred dance formed the basis of his training. All this was directed towards the reconciliation and union of the three basic functions of feeling, thinking and physical activity. It was during this period that he turned his attention to writing, producing three major works consisting of ten books divided into three series. The best known of the first series is *Beelzebub's Tales* and the second *Meetings With Remarkable Men*. His third work, *Life Is Real Only When I Am* is today published privately and used by those actively engaged in what is known as 'the Gurdjieff Work'.

The last period of his life was again a time of travelling with the establishing of groups in the USA. At the time of his death his writings were little known beyond the circle of his immediate followers, and his influence upon European thought and culture was negligible. Yet today those who are formally engaged in 'the work' can be numbered in many thousands and the influence of his teachings, especially on the young, is incalculable.

Kathleen Speeth, daughter of parents who were for many years prominent in the Gurdjieff work in the USA, attributes the growth of his influence to being 'in considerable measure due to the current resurgence of interest in Self Realization. This', she says, 'has led those suffering from what Jung called "Holy Neurosis" to seek for spiritual guidance wherever it is authentically presented' (*The Gurdjieff Work*). If she means that such spiritual guidance is authenticated by its moral impact upon those who accept Gurdjieff's assessment of human nature and follow his techniques of transformation, then without doubt this would be attested by those who are in 'the work'.

What then are the basics of Gurdjieff's teachings? The natural human being, he maintains, is a machine:

All its deeds, actions, words, thoughts, feelings, convictions, opinions and habits are the result of external influences and impressions. Out of itself the human being cannot produce a single thought, a single action. Everything it says, does, thinks and feels . . . all this just happens. (*In Search of the Miraculous*)

This human machine he sees as functioning through a multiplicity of mechanical 'I's. The 'I' that is in control of an individual's behaviour at any given moment is determined not by personal choice but rather by a reaction to circumstances and environment. The human being is therefore an automatic reactionary different from other animals in one respect only, namely that human beings are capable of knowing that a higher form of existence is possible and also of experiencing it. It is possible for human beings to find the will to true selfhood. When consciousness has begun to centre in the true self, the work of transformation can begin and there is an awakening to true humanity. This immediately communicates itself powerfully to others.

In *Meetings With Remarkable Men*, Gurdjieff illustrates this reality of communication. He tells a story related to him by a brother in a monastery he discovered in a remote part of Asia. It concerns the annual visit of two remarkable preachers to the monastery, Brother Arl and Brother Sez. Both made powerful impacts upon their listeners, but the nature of the impact of each differed in certain fundamentals. They spoke 'the same truths' which had a 'different effect' on members of the community. Brother Sez entranced his listeners with his eloquence and the beauty of his voice. Brother Arl's speech had almost the opposite effect, for his speech was indistinct and uncompelling, but the stronger the impression made each moment by the words of Brother Sez the more the impression evaporated until there remained ultimately in the hearer nothing at all. The case of Brother Arl was quite different. 'For', said the brother, 'at first what he says makes almost no impression. Later the gist of it takes on a definite form, and more and more each day is distilled into the heart and remains there for ever and ever.' It was the unanimous conclusion of the community that the sermons of Brother Sez proceeded only from his mind and therefore acted on their minds, whilst those of Brother Arl proceeded from his being and acted on their being.

It is impossible to examine the teachings of Gurdjieff without hearing again echoes of St Paul's cry, 'Awake you who sleep, and arise from the dead and Christ will give you life' (Eph. 5.14). Indeed the Gurdjieff system with its insistence upon the paralysis of human nature, helpless in the grip of reactionary forces, underlines the Pauline, Augustinian and Calvinistic view of human nature. For Gurdjieff the attainment of true Selfhood is possible but achieved at great cost. When asked about the nature of being a Christian he replied typically that 'hardly any have ever existed'.

Gurdjieff could be brutal and apparently unloving in his relationships with those who came to him for help. His attitude to everything unreal and hypocritical in human nature was uncompromising. He would penetrate immediately through all subterfuge, self-esteem and wrong motivation, and was apparently impervious to the opinion of others about him. Many stories are told of how with individuals and groups he would bring hidden and sometimes unconscious motivations to the surface, exposing pseudo-spirituality for what it was. He spoke often of the objective, as distinct from subjective, morality which he insisted most humans live by. Very few, he maintained, ever consider or approximate to this objective morality, and in the process of communicating this he himself appears to have broken every rule in the commonly accepted book of morals and ethics. It is possible to see him, and many do, as the exponent *par excellence* of 'situational ethics'.

Gurdjieff might well be described as 'the man nobody knew'. That he inspired utter devotion on the one hand and angry contempt on the other is not surprising. He must for ever remain an enigma. Yet there can be no doubt about what I would call the 'Gurdjieff dynamic' as it operates in Western society today, and it is with this dynamic that we are concerned. In his lifetime he acted as a mirror to many of those who came within his orbit, a mirror reflecting things as they really were. Today there is much evidence that the process continues. He was in many respects a John the Baptist calling people to repentance. But repentance (*metanoia*) was much more than a change in one's thinking. It must involve the totality of one's being. Spiritual awakening, he insisted, comes through shock. This may take place spontaneously through circumstances, it may be administered by a spiritual teacher, or self-administered. His teachings and techniques were directed to that end.

It is questionable whether we can improve upon his definitions of the 'human machine', and his insistence upon the necessity for awakening is in total accord with the New Testament. Characteristic of the man and his method is the story related to me by his one-time student, Pamela Travers, the author of *Mary Poppins*. 'Before he died,' she said, 'Mr Gurdjieff assured me that I was to be the sole transmitter of his authentic teachings after his death.' Then she added with a chuckle, 'He said that to at least a dozen people.'

One of his last acts therefore may be seen as a blow at the Gurdjieff cult which would be built around his name. He was an iconoclast to the last, and although a cult undoubtedly exists, his truly 'dynamic memorial' is his lasting contribution to the search for the true Self.

With Roberto Assagioli we move into an entirely different area of thought. Born in 1888, his education as a medical doctor and psychiatrist had its roots in the teaching of Freud. Before the First World War he formulated the concept of psychosynthesis, arguing that psychoanalysis was only a partial approach to an understanding of the human psyche. Assagioli's psychology of the human being includes the soul as well as Freud's libido. It includes the imagination as well as complexes, and the will as well as instinctual drives. Like Gurdjieff's his theories are expressed in practical work methods including a diversity of approaches to personal growth, encounter groups, the use of imagery and techniques of meditation. All these activities are unified around the concept of a real self at the core of each individual. This self (again like Gurdjieff) is capable of directing the harmonious development of all aspects of the personality. This operation of the true self gives access to genuine spiritual development.

Assagioli's book *Psychosynthesis* was first published in 1965.

It has since passed through many editions and constitutes a manual of principles and techniques. These, unlike those of Gurdjieff in relation to the religious establishment, have gained credibility amongst recognized leaders within the field of psychology.

Victor Frankl says, 'I regard psychosynthesis as a sound approach, particularly helpful as a counterweight to many of the one-sided trends which are presently so prevalent and predominant in the field of psychology.'

Albert Maslo sees psychosynthesis as of great value to those who are trying to help themselves towards self-growth and conscious experience.

Assagioli sums up his understanding of the nature of this self and the spiritual dimensions to which it relates as follows: 'We are using the word spiritual in its broader connotation which includes therefore not only specifically religious experience but all states of awareness . . . '

Today psychosynthesis exercises a growing influence on psychological thought and practice, and in its comparatively gentle step-by-step approach to self-realization speaks to those for whom the Gurdjieff work appears daunting and even threatening.

4

Experiential Wisdom

There are currently approximately two hundred Open Centres in the United Kingdom, bringing together people with widely differing approaches to discover the unifying principles behind our individual paths. All involved 'share the aim to be open to the truth'. What is quite clear from the acknowledged diversity of approaches and beliefs is that spiritual truth is not here conceived of as consisting of a set of immutable propositions received as a basis of faith, but rather it is to do with what F.C. Happold calls 'experiential wisdom'.

My visit to Iona had introduced me to the world of these Centres and I resolved to accept the invitation I had received whilst there to 'Come and see.' Some months had passed since my initial encounters with what for me was an entirely new world, a period during which I had begun to familiarize myself with many of the concepts by which I had felt bombarded during the conference. It was therefore with at least a little self-assurance that I set out to visit what I soon discovered to be a thriving Centre in the Gloucestershire countryside.

The venue was a seventeenth-century farmhouse. For many years neglected and derelict, the building was still in process of restoration. My first impression was of a hive of activity. Inside and outside of the building were dozens of mostly young people, some working on the land and others on the rebuilding of outhouses. Over all was an atmosphere of intense concentration. Then a bell clanged loudly from somewhere on the site and immediately silence reigned. Activities continued, but a sense of what I was later to hear described as 'self-remembering' was everywhere apparent. This continued for about ten minutes, after which we were summoned by a second bell to gather for meditation. Everybody moved in the direction of the great barn, which like the farmhouse itself had been both renovated and partly rebuilt.

It was later explained to me that the restoration had been done according to the laws of sacred geometry, a concept long recognized in the East as a science and undoubtedly reflected in the medieval cathedrals of Europe. The reason for this was a desire that the building should not simply house a static religious form, but rather that its proportions, its measurements and space should further the awakening of this new capacity for intuitive understanding, a faculty which it is believed is particularly in evidence in the new human being now beginning to appear.

My only perception during the meditation was that it was very easy to be still, not only physically but emotionally and mentally, in that building, and that the stillness was a corporate experience. There was, in the language of my own religious tradition, a real sense of fellowship.

During the midday meal I had an opportunity to become more closely aware of the fifty or so people staying at the farm. I found myself struggling to find a description of the group which would, for my own sense of security, satisfactorily describe them all. But this was quite impossible. Although most were in their teens and twenties there was a sprinkling of the middle-aged and over. If accents were a reliable indicator then class barriers had been transcended.

My sense of being more at home than at the beginning of the Iona conference was suddenly shattered by a question from an evidently intelligent young man sitting opposite. 'What do you think of Ibn Arabi?' I felt decidedly at a disadvantage, for never before had I heard the name. However, I covered my discomfort with subterfuge and said that I was looking forward to discovering more about him during the afternoon study session. This was a shot in the dark which fortunately accurately related to the programme; and it was in that session that I was introduced to the teachings of one whom I have since discovered to be revered by many as possibly the greatest mystic of all times.

Muhyiddin Ibn Arabi was born in Andalucia, Spain, in AD 1165. From the age of thirty-two he travelled extensively throughout the Muslim world, conversing with the greatest mystics, divines and philosophers of his day. Here it is interesting to note that he was a contemporary of the Christian mystics Francis of Assisi and Dominic. Although he himself was an eminent scholar and a teacher of some would say incomparable stature, he was an outspoken critic of religious and philosophical dogmatism and made many enemies among the theologians. He wrote five hundred books. Before he died in Damascus in 1240 he was greatly venerated and regarded as a saint.

The afternoon study session focused on one of Arabi's famous treatises: *Whoso Knoweth Himself Knoweth the Lord*. In his writings he uses a method of relentless logical deduction to bring the reader beyond logic to intuitive understanding, and his teaching finds powerful echoes in those of Meister Eckhart, born twenty years after his death. Arabi's treatise ends with the following hymn:

I know the Lord by the Lord, without doubt or wavering,
My essence is His essence in truth, without defect or flaw,
There is no becoming between these two, and my soul it
    is which manifests that secret.
And since I know myself without blending or mixture,
I attained to union with my beloved, without far or near.
I obtained gifts of the Lord of Affluence without
    upbraiding and without recrimination.
I did not lose to Him my soul, nor does it remain to the
    Lord of dissolution.

At the end of the two-hour session I was aware of what seemed like a paradoxical response. My head was spinning as a result of the intellectual stimulation but at the same time I found myself echoing the words of John Wesley: 'I felt my heart strangely warmed.'

The daily programme at the Centre was so planned that there were hardly any interim periods. One session immediately followed the other. This required a drastic change of attitude and functions. At one moment there would be a total preoccupation of the intellect with a particular area of study; the next there would be the demands of silence.

Silence, as already indicated, was an important aspect of the spiritual disciplines practised at the Centre. Soon after my arrival I commented on a strange pyramid-style wooden building set at some distance from the farmhouse. Large enough to provide a cell for one person only, this, I was told, housed people who wanted to go into seclusion, perhaps for a week or even a month.

Silence at the Centre was not an end in itself. It was a means directed towards very clear ends. The philosophy behind it was briefly as follows.

External silence is of value only in so far as it leads beyond itself and opens the door of the heart into interior silence. The conditions then become right for the opening of the inner ear. When once this has taken place it is possible to begin the process of becoming attuned to the sounds within the silence. This is parallel to the learning of a new language and requires both time and patience.

Far from being a vacuum, the silence to which the opening of the heart gives access contains many octaves of sound. Each is related to the other and the whole creates a pattern of harmony which expresses itself in and through those who are dying to their false selves and becoming alive to the true self. This state is also beyond the reach of those who are emotionally centred. Those who are thus bound can reach no further than sense perception and into what is commonly called the psychic world, which is but a reflection of human emotions.

My own spiritual tradition had taught me the value of silence and I had long been used to the exhortation at the beginning of a retreat to 'go into the silence'. Further than that I had never been instructed. Silence for me meant little more than space in which to attempt to follow the rarely-achieved aim of an uninterrupted train of thought.

As in all the Centres, meditation was an important feature of the daily programme. Each day began and ended in the great barn, with one hour's meditation. It is a curious fact that twenty-five years after the beginning of the meditation movement in the West there is still much confusion as to what is meant by the term.

The word 'meditation' comprehends three aspects of the total human being: the imagination, the intellect and the intuition. When the first of these takes precedence then the activity involved is described as creative; when the intellect is employed then the process is reflective. (Until recently the word 'meditation' has in the West been regarded as synonymous with 'reflection'). With the bringing into operation of the intuitive faculty, then meditation becomes contemplative. So we may speak of creative meditation, reflective meditation and contemplative meditation. At the Centre where I was a guest, the discipline of meditation was directed towards the awakening of the heart. It was therefore contemplative.

In the sharing sessions which sometimes followed meditation it was clear that in practice most people find that every meditation exercise involves in varying degrees elements of all three. For example the imagination might play an important part in the preparatory stage, when by building up in the imagination a picture of tranquillity a measure of physical, mental and emotional relaxation is achieved. This may then be followed by a brief reflection upon the intention of the meditation. The third stage is that of contemplation, when consciousness is focused on the still centre of the heart. It is at this stage that concentration may be aided by the image of light, or by the constant repetition of one word or *mantra* which does not necessarily have in itself any inherent meaning. Again for most people, especially in the early stages, the mind returns repeatedly from contemplation to reflection, and refocusing needs to be repeated again and again.

It is an undoubted fact that in the Western Church there is a long tradition of contemplative religious Orders, both in the Roman Catholic and Anglican Churches. Nevertheless, many contemplative communities have in practice followed chiefly the reflective meditation, and the word 'contemplative' has become the common description given to religious communities which are not active in the sense of involvement in teaching, nursing or other works of mercy. The reason for this lack of a strong contemplative consciousness is a deep reluctance to attempt to understand the faculty by which such contemplation becomes possible. This in spite of the fact that *gnosis* or knowledge is clearly part of the New Testament experience. The subsequent disappearance of this knowledge has run parallel to the Church's persistent rejection of *gnosis* under any form as a heresy. The fear of gnosticism, or a claim to special knowledge, runs deep within the psyche of Western Christendom and is reflected in the direction of theological studies as practised in all branches of the Christian Church. The New Testament experience is implicitly dismissed as an incipient heresy and therefore given no place within the framework of faith. This in spite of St Peter's exhortation to 'add to your faith knowledge' (2 Pet. 1.5). My own theological training had provided me with an inbuilt resistance to the word *gnosis*. I was reassured when the explanation was given that *gnosis* is to be understood as the wisdom of the heart.

Although the daily programme left no time for unplanned activity or even inactivity, there was a set time for recreation. This I found to be similar to that of the traditional religious communities of the Western Church. During this period set aside for the development of what some described – I thought rather ambiguously – as 'horizontal activities', I found the opportunity to discover something of the background and motivation of those visiting the farm. None were there for less than three days. This was an invariable rule. Less than that, I was told, did no more than satisfy intellectual curiosity, which could in fact mitigate against any real spiritual benefit. Many of those to whom I spoke said they were there because they wanted to make sense of life, to understand themselves and to find meaning and purpose. In answer to the question, 'How had they discovered this place?' most replied, 'On the grapevine of the alternative life style movement.'

Only a minority of those to whom I spoke had any contact with the Churches. Those who had saw no dichotomy between their allegiance to Christianity and their commitment to the aims of the Centre. 'You see,' explained the middle-aged wife of a Sussex estate manager, 'we are here to discover the essence of our religion, not to take on new patterns of faith. For the first time in my life I am beginning to appreciate the New Testament and the teachings of Jesus.' Then she added rather ruefully, 'I hope this will apply to my understanding of the Church also.'

This explanation was confirmed and reinforced by one of the founders of the Centre, a dynamic man in his late thirties. He described himself as 'a practising Anglican, somewhat at odds with my vicar'. He went on to explain that the Centre was not primarily concerned with patterns of belief but with working for inner awakening. 'Everybody must begin where they are. If this is within a pattern of belief, fine. If not, then work to discover your real potential.' Was it part of their function to seek to reconcile conflicting belief patterns, I asked. 'That', he asserted strongly, 'is a secondary operation. The first is to discover essential unity.'

'This', explained the focalizer at one of the group sessions, 'is what we would describe here as the new consciousness. It is to know that belief patterns and words, concepts and ideas, theological definitions, dogmas and doctrine are all articulations of the truth. They do not in themselves constitute the truth. Truth is the experience of reality in the present moment.'

The founder of the Centre was clearly something of a visionary and I asked him what he conceived to be its ultimate aim. I summarize his answer. It is to work for the coming to birth of human beings spiritually mature enough to live powerfully and effectively at points of intersection. These must be reconcilers in society. They would operate at points of tension between many paradoxes with values which are not commonly recognized as conventional or traditional. Asserting their continuity with the old, they would know themselves to belong to the new, children of a New Age, independent of, yet respecting all form. Seeking always to centre in the heart, they would touch that source by which the intellect is activated. Committed to a vision that goes far beyond individual spirituality, they recognize the infinite worth of each person; and looking into the future they would practise those disciplines which make it possible to live fully in the present moment, knowing that a true love for all humanity can proceed only from the knowledge that I AM. 'It is this knowledge', he concluded, 'that we work for here.'

5

Healers All

So far on our journey of investigation we have focused on movements operating outside of the churches and particularly in relation to the Open Centres. Early in my search I had become aware that not all New Age activities could be so easily categorized. Nowhere is this more apparent than in the field of healing.

I recall a dramatic confirmation of this. It was late one Saturday evening that I received a phone call from my bishop, who for some time had been ill with what had been diagnosed as a stomach ulcer. Clearly very excited, the bishop wanted me to know that he had been healed and that his healing had come through the ministrations of a lady with, as he put it, 'very great gifts of the spirit'. The lady in question was, by her own acknowledgement, a 'New Age' healer.

A few months later, after what the bishop clearly regarded as a miracle of divine healing, the lady was confirmed in his private chapel. All this was the more impressive as the bishop had himself long been prominent in the healing movement within the churches. From then on the sphere of the lady's work began to change for she now had episcopal recognition. Yet in character it remained the same.

My own introduction to non-medical healing had come almost twenty years before, in India. Miles from hospitals or qualified medical aid, missionaries frequently found themselves in situations where the New Testament injunction to lay hands on the sick and to offer the prayer of faith assumed a real and immediate significance; a ministry which many would testify was undoubtedly validated by physical and emotional healings. Later I was introduced to the Church's ministry of healing, a ministry which during recent years has undergone a remarkable revival in the Western Church.

If we are to acquire a balanced view of New Age healing, we must examine it in the context of the whole healing spectrum which now transcends many of the traditional barriers, both ecclesiastical and scientific.

At first sight its philosophy appears to be clear and simple. It stems from a recognition of the multidimensional nature of the human being and as such may claim to be part of the modern holistic approach to the problem of sickness and disease. It perceives that much of the disharmony in the human body is the expression of emotional, mental and spiritual disease, and that all valid treatment must go beyond the clearing up of symptoms and relate to the whole person.

Such a diagnosis of human need is consonant with much new thinking and practice within the medical profession. Nevertheless, closer investigation quickly reveals a morass of apparent contradictions and confusions. This is made very clear by Alice Bailey in what is regarded by many as a text book for the age, *Esoteric Healing*. In the Introduction she writes:

> When one enters the realm of healing, one enters a world of much esoteric knowledge, and of an infinity of conclusions, and one is faced with the formulations of many minds, who through the ages have sought to heal and to help. The why and the wherefore of disease have been the subject of endless investigations and speculations, and much deduction has been made as to the cures of such complaints: there has been also much formulation of methods, of techniques, of formulae, of prescription, of varied manipulations and of theories. All these serve to fill the mind with many ideas . . . some correct, some erroneous . . .

On a somewhat more positive note she goes on to say: 'All

l

initiates of the Ageless Wisdom are necessarily healers, though all may not heal the physical body. The reason for this is that all souls that have achieved any measure of true liberation are transmitters of spiritual energy.'

Yet there is clearly a distinctively New Age approach to healing in its assertion that today, as never before in human history, there are 'cosmic forces' available for healing, and that these forces may be called upon and utilized with very great benefit not only for individuals but for the healing of the nations, by those who are spiritually 'attuned' to this reality.

It is in the interpretation of the nature of these 'cosmic forces' that we move into areas of diversity and sometimes credulity. For there are no commonly agreed answers and no clear criteria by which the 'energy' is to be authentically defined or assessed. At one end of the scale are those who interpret it as an impersonal force latent within all human beings, powerfully present in a few. Many see this in evolutionary terms and relate what is happening to the concept of a current 'leap epoch', with new energies welling up within the human psyche. At the other end of the scale are those who, whilst having no particular religious affiliations, claim their capacity to heal as a divine gift dispensed by the Almighty according to his will. In between these two is a whole range of interpretation. The adjectives 'psychic', 'spiritual', 'magnetic', 'faith' and 'charismatic' are all used to categorize the activity. Some claim to be agents and instruments of healers from 'the other side'. Often these are declared to be well-known medical practitioners who after death continue their healing work through suitable mediums. These people invariably link their healing power to that of clairvoyance, by which they discern the needs of a particular patient. Many refer to themselves as 'sensitives' preferring this to the term 'spiritualist'.

During my attendance at the Iona conference I had witnessed several healing sessions. They bore remarkable resemblance to what in certain Christian 'renewal' circles is described as 'soaking prayer'. The patient was seated on a chair in the centre of a small circle of healers. Following a period of silent prayer and 'attunement', those members of the circle who so wished laid hands upon the one seeking healing. This laying on of hands lasted for about five minutes, during which those taking part would move their hands to different parts of the patient's body. The session ended with more prayer, both silent and audible.

Does it work? From this and subsequent participation in similar events my general impression is that almost invariably the patient experiences a general sense of well-being and a resurgence of vital energy. It is also true that emotional and physical healing do take place. Beyond that a fair and accurate assessment of results is impossible. Claims are made for the complete cure of a great number of illnesses. Medical opinion is divided. A few doctors are prepared to recognize that the practice has a place alongside scientific medicine. Others dismiss all such cures as 'spontaneous' healing.

Some healers combine the use of their 'gift' with osteopathy, acupuncture or reflexology, so moving into the field of supplementary medicine. Undoubtedly the combination of the two widens considerably the field of credibility and recognition.

'Absent healing' also has an important part to play. This may be done either by individuals or groups. Behind this practice is the belief that 'energy' follows thought and that the unselfish directing or channelling of energy can bring healing to the recipient. Various techniques are employed to facilitate the process. If it constitutes a group activity, then quite frequently those taking part may visualize the sick person as though he or she were actually present within the circle. Sometimes the patient is 'held in the light'. The members of the group may imagine themselves to be laying hands upon those for whom they are concerned. As will be seen, such healing is being exercised within the setting of creative meditation where visualization and imagination play an important role. Traditional prayer groups for healing, found in many parishes throughout the country, may use a language very different from those set up for the purpose of 'absent healing', but the function of the group is determined not by the language used or the label applied, but by the operation of those taking part.

In the case of absent healing on the part of an individual healer, then the sick person is asked to 'tune in' at a particular time. In true esoteric healing the energy is directed to the *chakras* (described in Chapter One) and a process of what is described as 'balancing the energies' may be undertaken. This is described in detail in Alice Bailey's *Esoteric Healing*.

Does all this relate in any way to the Church's ministry of healing? Are these all expressions of the same dynamic operating through a great variety of individuals and groups? In making an objective assessment, the same criteria must be applied to each. To do this we need to examine the origin and true essence of Christian healing.

There can be no doubt concerning the attitude of Jesus toward human sickness and disease. He treated them unequivocally as alien to the divine plan and purpose for humanity. His unique mission was to declare through his person a new dimension of living, the opening up of a new potential on a universal scale hitherto unknown. This dimension he called 'the Kingdom of God', and the signs that the Kingdom had come were seen, to use the language of the New Testament in 'the casting out of evil spirits and the curing of disease'.

This was fundamental to the ministry of Jesus. Yet it is important to discern the true nature of this healing ministry, for here we find the key to healing in its totality. It issued out of unlimited compassion and expressed itself in perfect knowledge. It was never limited to the relief of symptoms, nor concerned exclusively with the physical. It was a ministry to the whole person.

An example of this may be seen in the Gospel story of the healing of a paralysed man (Luke 5.18–26). For Jesus spoke not to his apparent need, which was of course the paralysis, but to his essential need. To do this he used the words, 'Your sins are forgiven you.' Immediately the healing process was set in motion, and the man picked up his bed and walked away.

During the period recorded in the New Testament, documented healings of every kind were experienced by the followers of Jesus. These were the 'signs' which he had promised would attend their work. They continued for almost two centuries, but gradually as the Church became increasingly preoccupied with speculations concerning the nature of Jesus rather than the truth which had manifested so powerfully through him, the healing dynamic generally disappeared.

So, with some exceptions, as in the case of those powerful surges of spiritual life which accompanied the birth of the religious Orders and revival movements, the healing ministry of the Church disappeared until the great awakenings which began towards the end of the nineteenth century.

The most spectacular of the movements appeared in the birth of the Pentecostal Churches. These came into being as a result of a revival movement, an upsurge of energy which swept through the churches of Scandinavia, Britain, the USA and then the mission fields of the East. This movement constituted a rediscovery of what the New Testament describes as 'the gifts of the Spirit'. Prominent among them was the gift of healing. At about the same time there were less spectacular but equally significant developments within the more conservative churches.

The holistic movement had begun. Groups began to form within the Churches, sometimes part of an early ecumenical activity, with the aim of bringing together doctors, psychiatrists, clergy and social workers in an interdisciplinary approach to the problems of wholeness and health. Guilds such as The Guild of Health were formed with the express purpose of re-establishing the ministry of healing which it was now recognized constituted an essential part of the early Church's gospel.

The early part of this century witnessed in the Western world the rise of some outstanding individuals possessing outstanding powers of healing. In Britain the most remarkable of these was

Dorothy Kerin, who as a young woman was instantaneously cured of a combination of diseases which by medical standards were incurable. Her subsequent lifelong dedication to re-establishing the Church's lost healing ministry and relating it to Orthodox medicine is an impressive story. Her significance in the revival of healing is to be seen in the context of the now widespread reaching out towards a wholeness of living which had largely disappeared from post-industrial society. Dorothy Kerin's life work pointed far beyond physical healing, beyond the clearing up of symptoms, to healing at a deeper level.

That this deeper level was anything but clear to many who were carried along on the wave of almost hysterical enthusiasm for physical healing in the twenties and thirties, is evidenced by the disillusionment which followed the great healing missions so popular at the time.

In his book *Wounded Spirits*, published in 1962, Leslie Weatherhead describes the dangers which he saw then:

> In such an atmosphere symptoms often temporarily disappear, and false hopes are given birth which die a death devastating indeed to the mind of the patient. Unless the deep underlying cause of the disease is dealt with . . . even if the symptoms permanently disappear the unconscious mind will express its continuing disease in another symptom much harder to cure.

In my experience the failure to get at real causes and to treat only symptoms is common right across the healing board, whether it be at the hands of overworked physicians, undiscerning clergy or misguided New Age healers.

During my time as Warden of the Burrswood Home of Healing founded by Dorothy Kerin, I recall a clear example of this. A patient who could walk only with the aid of two sticks due to an arthritic condition of the joints, and who suffered considerable pain, returned from the laying on of hands at the communion rail declaring that she could now walk unaided. The improvement lasted for about a week, when she suddenly

reverted to her original condition. Unable to cope with a difficult domestic situation to which she had returned, she unconsciously retreated into an illness which was clearly psychosomatic. The laying on of hands – the significance of which we shall
examine later – had brought about a partial and temporary
improvement.

In recent years the Charismatic movement, which is in fact
the second wave of the Pentecostal revival but now manifesting
within the traditional Churches, has done much to revive consciousness of healing power. In its emphasis on the psychic gifts
it bears a remarkable resemblance in all but language to the
New Age phenomenon.

Indeed, as we look at the many and varied facets of New
Age healing we find many parallels within the ecclesiastical
structures. Both may be seen as an expression of hitherto sup-
pressed creative energies, which when released give birth to
little-understood faculties latent within the human psyche.
Dorothy Kerin, with her well-attested capacity for 'seeing into'
the motivations of those who came to her for help, would
certainly have explained her gifts in terms very different from
those of Harry Edwards, her Spiritualist contemporary. Yet
who is to say that the motivations of one were higher than
the other's? Each achieved spectacular successes through the
exercise of super-normal powers. Neither took credit for themselves, but repeatedly maintained that they were but unworthy
channels of divine power. As far as can be judged, the results
of both ministries in terms of physical healings, changed lives
and grateful recipients are comparable.

Traditionally the Church has exercised its ministry chiefly
through the laying on of hands. This is sometimes accompanied
by anointing with oil. Sensitives claim to be able to see energy
streaming from the hands of a healer during a healing session.
And what of this energy? Is that conveyed by the minister
of religion at the altar rail different in kind from the power
transmitted in a New Age sanctuary with its eclectic signs and
symbols?

It is commonly attested by patients of both Church and non-Church healers that at the time hands are laid upon them they experience sensations of heat, sometimes of great intensity, travelling throughout the body. As Leslie Weatherhead points out in *Wounded Spirits*, this heat transference is a well-known phenomenon associated with 'odic force'. He devotes a whole chapter to examining the nature of this force. It is hard to define, for it cannot be scientifically verified. Nevertheless it is an undoubted factor integral to the use of hand-healing.

Odic force was first identified by Carl Reichenbach who lived in Stuttgart in the early nineteenth century. His researches into magnetism led him to a discovery of what he describes as emanations which proceed from a number of substances but more particularly from the human body. In some people these emanations are very powerful indeed. Dr Weatherhead writes: 'A definition of odic force is difficult and I can only offer that put forward by Reichenbach . . . He defines it as a "current of energy which emanates from certain organic and inorganic bodies, including human bodies, plants, magnets, crystals . . ." '

In passing, it is worth noting that within certain New Age groups, healing through crystals, which are credited with near-magical properties, plays a central role.

To recognize this as a reasonable explanation of the common experience of those at the receiving end of healing activity in no way diminishes the element of divine activity. It does, however, bring into question the sometimes enthusiastic equation made between healing heat and the Holy Spirit! It also underlines the observation of Peter in the Acts of the Apostles (10.34), that 'God is no respecter of persons.'

Wherever human beings move consciously away from introverted self-concern and give themselves to a greater good, here true prayer is being offered, and such activity is truly in Christ's name.

This we see epitomized in the exercise of a healing ministry by Peter and John in the Acts of the Apostles (3.1–9), '. . . A

man who had been crippled from birth . . . when he saw Peter
and John asked for charity . . . Peter said, "What I have I give
you. In the name of Jesus Christ of Nazareth, walk." . . . He
sprang up, stood on his feet and walked.'

The apostles were perfectly attuned to the divine purpose
which had manifested so powerfully in their midst. They were
completely aligned to the Spirit of healing released among the
disciples. Because of this alignment they were, as are all who
so align themselves, channelling the truth as manifested in
Jesus. They were therefore acting and operating in His name.
The words themselves are not to be seen as authenticating the
action. The reverse is true. For as Jesus himself warned, 'Many
will say to me, "Lord, Lord, did we not prophesy in your name,
cast out devils in your name and in your name perform many
miracles?" Then I will tell them, "I never knew you"' (Matt.
7.21–3).

It is this same principle which must be applied if we are to
penetrate the confusion which spreads right across the healing
scene. It is necessary to be quite clear that spiritual realities
are not determined by language, and that discernment is of
fundamental importance if we are to distinguish between the
real and the unreal. We remind ourselves of the words of Jesus
himself: 'By their fruits ye shall know them' – not by their
labels, whether self-chosen or applied by others.

All healing which is the exercise of personal power, motivated by less than concern for the divine plan and purpose for
all humanity, and outside the context of love, is *psychic*, for it
has no more than a limited transitory and human dimension.
No healing is truly *spiritual* if unrelated to the source of spiritual
living; and regardless of the context within which it operates,
healing is *divine* if it is related to the divine plan for the restoration of harmony and wholeness.

A question frequently asked in connection with healing is,
'How important is faith?' We turn again to the ministry of
Jesus. If faith is defined as belief in the divine will and power
to heal, then the answer is clear. In every situation where

Jesus healed, such faith was somewhere inherent. Sometimes it operated within the needy individual, at others it was exercised by friends or interested parties. On occasions it was active within a corporate situation where the need existed, i.e. it permeated the thought patterns and processes, the very atmosphere, where Jesus was working. Conversely, when faith was entirely absent, 'because of their unbelief he could do no mighty works'. Always it was greater than a credal statement. Its essential ingredient was receptivity.

Referring once more to Leslie Weatherhead's *Wounded Spirits*, we find wise guidelines as we look for authenticity:

> I am sure that there are many energies in the Universe as yet untapped which God means us to use to make wounded spirits whole. I want to help release them without descending to magic or superstition.

6

Why the Church?

Many times during my journey of investigation I have been asked, 'Why the Church?' For those posing the question, both the origin of the Church and its *raison d'être* seemed quite obscure.

The result of this for me has been a reappraisal of my own spiritual heritage and an examination of those historical processes which have given birth to the ecclesiastical structures where my faith had been nurtured. More than that, it has pinpointed for me those contemporary movements of convergence which transcend many of the traditional boundaries.

During this period of examining and assessing my religious roots, I was touring the churches of Brazil and was invited to visit a temple belonging to one of the many eclectic religious groups which abound in that country. At the focal point of the community's religious activity, and presenting very much the appearance of a museum, was a vast collection of articles – pictures of Red Indian chiefs, statues of saints long dead, amulets, crucifixes and various other objects of veneration. The total effect was to pull one's attention back into events long since gone and generally forgotten. The crystallization of a dynamic which had been important in the very shaping of Brazil was everywhere apparent. This dynamic, it seemed, had moved on; only the object of the cult remained. For me this was a striking illustration of the distinction between dynamic and cult, and the importance of distinguishing between the two in the context of religion.

A dynamic signifies movement, a flowing current, a creative energy, a life-giving process. The cult is static; it is fundamentally different. Nevertheless the one cannot exist without the other. Dynamic precedes cult, and of necessity gives birth to cult by the very law of manifestation.

In the history of religion an invariable law appears to work. A dynamic is seen to operate within the context of a culture, a society, a nation. The ultimate reality from which the dynamic proceeds is known as God. In Christian terminology the attribute of Fatherhood is given to the ultimate reality, Son to the principle of manifestation, and Spirit to the dynamic. The manifestation of the dynamic is usually in and through an individual who is seen to be moving spiritually in advance of his fellows – obvious examples are Gautama the Buddha, Jesus Christ, and Mohammed. The power of the dynamic and its particular kind of energy is manifested primarily through the being of the particular individual, and has immediate impact upon other individuals and upon society. From this source the 'beingness' of individuals and groups is profoundly affected. It is as if a process of internal combustion is generated. Like calls to like, and an enormous potential and power with an authentic moral content is released, producing a sense of unified identity within humanity. The function of the dynamic is therefore seen to be to generate and transform. Such is the dynamic. The law of manifestation follows. This leads to crystallization in the form of a cult.

In general terms in the history of religion the crystallization follows a clear pattern: (a) in the form of scriptures and written traditions: (b) in ecclesiastical systems or clearly distinguishable societies, as for example in Judaism and Islam. So the dynamic gives way to cult. The two may coexist harmoniously or otherwise at intermittent periods, either in individual or group situations. Nevertheless the two are separate; the one is the esoteric, the other the exoteric face of religion. The former, which has to do with essence, is one wherever and whenever it operates. The second is seen in diversity, a diversity provided by the particular vehicles of manifestation, that is the type of humanity, cultural environment, period of history, and so on. The dynamic is one, the cult is manifold.

This in broad outline is the pattern in relation to religion in general. How do these principles relate to the Christian Church in particular? Here it is of course easy to take a superficial view, to be cynical and to see this universal phenomenon as the opium of the people, a tool of right-wing reactionary governments, an initiator of civil wars or, coming home to this country and the established Church, simply the middle classes at prayer.

For a true perspective we need to look first at the Christian beginning, at one of the most powerful, dynamic manifestations in the history of the human race, operative in and through Jesus of Nazareth. Here we observe a dynamic which two thousand years later is still powerfully operating within a great diversity of human beings. The initial impact of the dynamic was incalculable and in two thousand years of subsequent history the operation of the principles we have examined has been beyond measure – the cult in terms of universal influence, and the dynamic as an evolutionary and indeed cosmic force.

We have already noted that both cult and dynamic have their function and place in history. It is the function of the cult to preserve and restrain within society. How has this operated through Christianity? The Church has at best provided, primarily in the Western world but also significantly in the East, ethical systems which have become the basis for national and international laws. This it has done by the transmission of truth at its exoteric level, through its ecclesiastical systems and through the Scriptures. In the West it has provided the basis for a civilization which until now has given communities, societies and nations cohesiveness, unity and stability. Most significantly in spiritual terms, it has provided in its dogmas, doctrines, formularies and creeds, and above all in its Scriptures, 'truths' capable when rightly understood and assimilated of manifesting in transforming power. What of the dynamic during the two thousand years of ecclesiastical history, and what measure of consciousness has the Church of these realities? At worst she has identified herself and her ecclesiastical being as the dynamic, and this has given rise to rampant triumphalism. At best her awareness has given her perspectives to see the action of God beyond herself, and to further this action in works of compassion, and in the initiation of movements for renewal and reform. Sadly the former has been nearer the norm; and even when the dynamic has been acknowledged and given space, attempts to trap, hold and control it within the cult have followed. So organism has given way to organization.

Again and again in the history of the Church this action is repeated. In the Roman Catholic Church, recognition of the dynamic gave birth to the great religious Orders. Within Protestantism it gave rise to renewal movements which crystallized into denominations. These in their turn, as they touched the dynamic, gave life to new movements. So diversity of cults was established even within Christendom; and as preoccupation with the cult developed, so the dynamic, unobserved, withdrew and moved on.

A few great souls have kept allied to the dynamic throughout a lifetime. These are the ones who shape the history of humanity. They are rare indeed. Few of the stature of St Francis of Assisi have appeared within two thousand years, and the sad fact is that their followers, whilst protesting their undeviating and undying loyalty to the vision of the great ones, in the end become preoccupied with propagating the cult and are again lost to the dynamic. In the words of the great Dominican mystic, Meister Eckhart, 'He who seeks God under settled forms lays hold on the form while missing the God within.' Nevertheless the particular dynamic which gave birth in cultic form to Christendom is today still operating with power. How may this be seen within the cultic forms?

Since the industrial revolution very great changes have taken place within the social consciousness of Western man. As a result education, medicine, and social responsibility all reflect these changes. Not so apparent are the parallel changes in religious consciousness which, although reflected in New Age activity, are only just becoming apparent in the Churches. Nevertheless, during the second half of this century powerful movements of thought and renewal have profoundly affected the Churches of the West. These developments may be seen as preparing the way for even greater changes.

In the 1950s and 1960s a great deal was heard about 'religionless Christianity'. This was popularized by men such as Harvey Cox in the USA, particularly by his book *The Secular City*. This movement had the effect of helping many to see God at work in the technological world of the twentieth century, and in the whole of life. God was ceasing to be remote. He was seen to be related as much to the present life of industrial Europe as to the pastoral scenes of the Bible. The industrial revolution was recognized not as something to escape from, but rather as part of the divine economy. God was drawing nearer to the world as it now exists.

Almost at the same time came the book by Bishop John Robinson, *Honest to God*, with its emphasis on God not as a Being above and beyond humanity, but as the very ground of man's being. So great have been the changes in thought since those days that it is difficult today to appreciate the furore which followed the book's publication in 1963. At the time it evoked tremendous publicity, reaction from those who saw it as a direct attack upon revealed truth, and response from those who were struggling to free themselves from the old anthropomorphic images of God. For many the book did not tell them something new; rather it brought into their consciousness that which for long they had known intuitively. It took the lid off the religious situation and brought a great release. With it came a significant shift in the Church's consciousness of the divine. God was no longer somewhere 'out there'. He was 'deep down within'.

It was during this period that 'situational ethics' burst upon the Church. Serious and eminently respectable religious thinkers put forward the proposition that very few things are in themselves intrinsically good or bad, but that circumstances determine the morality or otherwise of an action; the only ultimate criterion being that of charity. Once more there was reaction and response. Reaction came from those who saw this as an opening of the door to sheer licence and debauchery and a final jettisoning of the Christian ethic, and response from those who saw it as in accord with the authentic spirit of Christ. The judgemental face of the divine being was surrendering to one of compassion.

Parallel to this came the Death of God movement, claiming that God, as popular belief had for centuries conceived him, was dead and done for. The God who had simply filled in the gaps left by science and who operated from over and above the world was finally buried.

Then came the very questioning of God's maleness. Liturgies and translations of the Scriptures which failed to reflect the feminine in the Godhead came under scrutiny, and were found by an increasing number to be wanting. So here, in the space of about twenty-five years, powerful movements of thought became manifest, questioning the traditions of centuries in regard to the Church's image of itself, concepts of God and ethical and moral standards. There has in fact been a tremendous loosening up, a deconditioning process, a questioning of assumptions once thought to be inviolable.

At the same time there have been movements for renewal operating within the life of the Church. These have been concerned not primarily with changing patterns of thought, but rather with the experience of the psycho-spiritual, both corporate and individual.

The first of these is known as the Liturgical Movement, a renewal and reformation of worship which began around the turn of the century, largely as a result of biblical studies within the Roman Catholic Church. Centres such as the ancient Benedictine monastery at Maria Laach in Germany played a very significant part in the movement. Broadly speaking, this constituted a rediscovery of the Church as the 'people of God', not as buildings, or as a priestly caste with the laity as obedient servants, but as a community with the celebration of Mass or the Holy Communion as the great corporate act of the people of God, Sunday by Sunday. The effect of this has been to change the whole face of the Roman Catholic Church in a way that Luther was never able to do, with powerful overspills into the Anglican and Protestant Churches.

Its culmination was in the Second Vatican Council, of which it had been the great forerunner. It took half a century of liturgical renewal to make possible the arrival of a Pope John XXIII and such a Council. When this happened the doors were thrown open for a further movement, namely the Roman Church's participation in the Ecumenical Movement. This is now truly ecumenical for it embraces all the major Churches of Christendom. So great barriers between separated and often competing Christians have been demolished, and dogma and doctrine have begun to be seen in a new perspective, that of charity.

In the late 1960s there burst upon the Church the most dramatic of the renewal movements: the Charismatic experience. In an unbelievably short period this renewal of the early Church's experience of the psychic 'gifts of the Spirit,' pre-eminent amongst them speaking in tongues and gifts of healing, has made its impact on all the major Churches of the Western world. Its effect in terms of breaking down conventional Christian behaviour patterns and in creating loving, sharing communities should not be underestimated. To recognize the short-comings of this movement in its general lack of awareness of the nature of the energies it has generated does not diminish its significance. For many it has proved to be a necessary stage in the growth of self-awareness. The charismatic experience, when it leads on to what St Paul describes as 'the more excellent way of charity', can be profoundly significant as a transition from religious conventionalism to the opening of the heart and into that path which the New Age consciousness perceives as 'experiential wisdom'. It is significant that many who experience charismatic release, both through New Age impulses and from within the Churches, eventually seek the contemplative path.

In like manner the Ecumenical Movement, which within the Christian world has transcended barriers of dogma and doctrine and conceded, at least in theory, the pre-eminence of charity above all things, may be seen as the precursor of something greater. It is arguable that unless it is to founder in its present cul-de-sac it must move in this greater direction. Ecumenism has prepared the way for the coming of what F.C. Happold calls 'intersection'.

Intersection may be described as standing at a point between two worlds which at the level of rational thought are in contradiction, but which at a deeper level are seen to be one. An example of this may be seen throughout history in the experience of the mystics. Emerging from the heart of all the great religions, they find themselves within conflicting belief patterns which superficially divide them. In their common experience of the divine love and their touching of reality they are united.

One of the great forerunners of intersection was Simone Weil, the French-Jewish resistance fighter in France during the Second World War. Her perception of the Christ who fills all things made it possible for her to enter into an exclusive commitment to him. Therefore, born a Jew she died in the Jewish religion, yet fully and sacrificially committed to the Christ who transcends the barriers.

In *Religious Faith and Twentieth Century Man*, Happold describes Simone Weil's experience:

I first came across the word [intersection] in Simone Weil's *Waiting for God*. In this autobiographical letter she tells how, as an adolescent, though remaining within the Christian inspiration she concluded that the problem of God was one which was insoluble for the human mind. So she decided to leave it alone. Through the profound mystical experience which she describes she was drawn to Christ. She, however, refused to be baptized into the Catholic Church because she felt that Christianity, while Catholic by right, was not so in fact. It was not a truly incarnated Christianity; too much was outside it. Therefore 'Now my heart has been transported for ever, I hope, into the Blessed Sacrament exposed on the altar,' she wrote. 'Yet I should betray the truth, that is the aspect of truth which I see, if I left the point where I have been since my birth, at the intersection of Christianity and everything that is not Christian.'

It is the very experience of intersection, often entered into quite unconsciously, that is now operating at the parish level within the Churches. Of this I was given a striking example during a recent visit to an Anglican convent. The Superior asked me if I would give some time to one of the sisters whom she described as having a pastoral problem. The sister explained to me that she had for some time been building up a weekly meeting for contemplative prayer and meditation. The group had grown rapidly in numbers and in its capacity to share in silence 'at a very deep level'. Most of the hour-long meeting was spent in silence and it was only after this silent sharing that there was any conversation. 'My difficulty is,' explained the sister, 'that I recently discovered that one or two people who have recently joined the group, and who are deeply spiritual, now tell me that they are not sure that they would label themselves as Christians; yet if to be heart-centred is to be Christ-centred then clearly we are on the same path.' The perplexed sister went on to say that the newcomers' reluctance to give themselves labels was not because they were in any way un-Christian, but rather because they felt that the spiritual awareness which was undoubtedly theirs they held in common with others whose belief patterns were different.

The good sister was by no means alone in facing this problem. I recall conducting an Insight Retreat in New South Wales for a group of about thirty people. At the beginning of the day we decided not to follow the common practice of introducing ourselves at the outset, thus acquiring for all participants safe labels and recognizable pigeon-holes. Few of those taking part had any knowledge of the rest of the retreatants. During the day there was considerable opportunity for sharing insights and articulating the understanding which had come to the group through the use of movement, music and sound. The sense of oneness and participation in a common experience was very profound. Then at the close of the day we revealed our identities. They ranged from self-styled agnostics to Roman Catholic clergy.

While I was in the course of writing this book, three Buddhist monks arrived one evening at the door of the Priory where I live. Our Order endeavours, in the words of St Benedict, to 'receive all guests as Christ Himself', and the community were delighted to welcome them.

During the twenty-four hours in which they remained as our guests the monks joined with us in meditation, shared with us in the offices and ate with us in the refectory. No one in the community had any doubt but that we had also shared 'fellowship in Christ'.

Such experiences are salutary reminders of Christ's words: 'Not everyone who calls me Lord shall enter into the kingdom of heaven but those who do the will of my Father' (Matt. 7.21). Yet they are more than just reminders, for they must compel us to a careful examination of the New Testament teaching concerning the nature of truth.

7

The Nature of Truth

Soon after my ordination to the priesthood I came into sharp encounter with a member of the local Kingdom Hall of Jehovah's Witnesses. A man gentle and kindly by nature, I also recognized him to be a relentless missionary. His natural courtesy brought him to the parsonage, where he introduced himself as a 'Bible Witness'.

Following the visit he examined the literature displayed on a table at the entrance to the church. This, according to his understanding of the Scriptures, was 'erroneous'. The first part of our meeting had been friendly enough, but the discovery of the literature led us both very quickly to a different level of interaction. His innate goodness and warmth were immediately subjected to his religious convictions and I assumed the role of a 'defender of the faith.'

Had it not been for the insuperable nature of the theological barriers between us, I have no doubt that we could have become good friends. Our faith in God prevented it! The meeting ended with a mutual bombarding with passages from the one Bible in which we both placed our faith. The encounter only confirmed us in our separate boxes.

How very different was this encounter from the coming together at an entirely different level of operation so often experienced in the Open Centres I have visited in recent years.

What exactly was happening, and where in that situation lay 'truth'? Both protagonists in the battle of words which characterized our meeting were contenders for the truth. Yet the truth as each saw it was apparently irreconcilable. Not only this, but our conscious level of communication, which was that of intellectual combat, did not operate in isolation from another more powerful but subtle form of interaction. The disputation resulted in an intellectual impasse, as well as a deepening of mutual antipathy and a reinforcement of antagonism. The engagement had in fact fertilized a seed-bed for the nurturing of those very forces which the two systems of theology professed to oppose.

Nevertheless the encounter between us had taken place according to a generally accepted pattern of communication and within a commonly held concept of the nature of truth. Each of us had entered the debate with two assumptions: (a) that of a deposit of truth to be communicated at all costs; and (b) that such communication must be made in terms of intellectual propositions. This was our common ground and constituted the agreed rules. It was upon these assumptions that our respective theological training had been founded.

It is against this concept of truth and such methods of communication that today's spiritual revolt is taking place. The rejection is by a generation which perceives the frequent dichotomy between verbal and non-verbal communication. It is a rejection by those who cannot with integrity give credence to words divorced from a more powerful and significant level of operation.

My experience at the conference on Iona had been very different. When I had endeavoured to engage a number of the young people in debate about the diversity of our beliefs they responded very disarmingly, 'But it is you we want to know, not what you believe.'

For many young people today it is truth as it proceeds from 'beingness' that is important. This is one of the reasons why Buddhist spirituality has such a strong appeal in the Western world, with its insistence that 'Only by work on oneself can one truly help others.'

During my time on the staff of Coventry Cathedral I was

strikingly reminded of how truth at a level other than that of the intellect can be powerfully conveyed. I had recommended for Lenten reading the book *The Phenomenon of Man* by the priest-scientist Teilhard de Chardin. On reflection it seemed to me that such an erudite volume might prove too much for some in the congregation, and I awaited the end of Lent and reports back with trepidation. My fears proved groundless when members of the community one after another testified along the lines that 'The book was not easy to assimilate intellectually, but it communicated something very powerful and good from the author, to which I found myself intuitively responding.'

Such powerful participation in the truth at this level may take place even in the context of profound theological differences. This was recently demonstrated for me by two visitors to the Priory. 'We have come', they volunteered, 'to find out what you are about.' My conditioned response was to make a quick assessment of their appearance and manner, which resulted in the conclusion that they had come to enter into verbal debate. I was wrong. They wished only to be left alone to move around the house and to spend time in prayer. Before leaving they asked to speak to me. They represented a fundamentalist body, yet clearly they abounded in charity. 'Your forms of worship are quite different from ours, as is your language, but we recognize the spirit of what this place is about. We are one with you and feel drawn to come again.'

It is because of a quickening of perception at this deeper level that many who are travelling a spiritual path find unacceptable the idea of submission to either a biblical or an ecclesiastical authority without reference to an inner resonance. Submission to the truth in this sense is felt to be a denial of integrity and something divorced from spiritual awakening. Yet this attitude is not to be dismissed as either anti-intellectual or anarchist. Rather it is a desire for recognition of the 'whole truth'.

That truth is many-faceted is illustrated by a story from the East, of a king who determined that he could and would make all his subjects speak and practise nothing but the truth. At the gate of the capital city he erected a gallows and appointed a day when all his subjects should report at the gates. 'Each one', he declared, 'will be questioned carefully. Those who tell the truth will be admitted, those who lie will be hanged.' On the appointed day a wise old man advanced boldly to the gates. 'Where are you going?' demanded the guard. 'I am going', the old man replied deliberately, 'to be hanged.' 'I don't believe you,' replied the guard. 'Then hang me,' said the wise man. 'But', said the puzzled guard, 'if I hang you for lying, I shall have made what you say come true.' 'Exactly,' came the reply. 'Now you know what truth is, your truth!'

New Age Centres bear witness to the fact that a generation has arrived which has an entirely new approach to learning. Educational techniques which appear to by-pass the intuitive faculty are rejected, and the catechetical approach to learning is increasingly unacceptable. It is a recognition of 'their' truth that many are asking for. Whatever explanation is given to this development, and it is probable that it can only be accurately assessed by a later generation, the evidence suggests that there is substance to the claim that the intuitive faculty is more active than has been known in previous generations. The significance of this in promoting religion is important, particularly in relation to preaching and evangelism. Any dichotomy between that which is being proclaimed and that which communicates itself from the being of the proclaimer, is sometimes painfully apparent to a generation whose perceptions go beyond the apparent to the real.

In the face of this the age of oratory is passing, and its effects are minimal. Passion and power are no longer recognized as constituting or increasing authority. Whereas for previous generations the proclamation of the Word, that is the sermon, was a final authority, for this New Age words are assuming a new significance. They are either a confirmation or a denial of that which is already being communicated and projected at a deeper, non-verbal level.

What then is the function of religion in relation to the search for knowledge of the truth? First of all it is necessary to recognize that the ecclesiastical systems and the Scriptures pertain not primarily to knowledge but to faith. Sacred books and community structures provide frameworks of faith. Within these frameworks the search for knowledge may be pursued. The forms themselves do not constitute the truth. Both Church and Scriptures contain guidelines for the search. Truth defined in this way relates to our cerebral capacity to acquire and accumulate information. Truth in relation to the knowledge of the heart, as we have seen, may be defined as that which in a given situation awakens to ultimate reality, no more no less. 'That' can never be identified with static form or a doctrinal definition. It cannot exist as an intellectual proposition appropriate to all situations. Nor can it be propagated as such. Verbal crystallizations may express and confirm the experience of reality. To this particular function of the Scriptures we shall return later.

To identify the verbal transmission, however venerable and revered throughout history, as that which as such awakens to reality, leads only to confusion. It merely increases the supply of information and reshapes the thought processes. Such reshaping frequently superimposes a particular religious form on an unchanged human machine.

To many people educated in a particular religious tradition, the assimilation of 'truth' has consisted of a systematic pumping of information into a cerebral reservoir. The brain thus becomes a veritable storehouse of information which far outstrips experience and is totally unrelated to real 'being'. For such the theological and biblical information received eventually becomes a burden grievous to be borne, gives birth to cynicism and mitigates powerfully against inner awakening.

Congregations conditioned in this way by what is in effect indoctrination may, unless carefully prepared, find sudden propulsion into 'real situations' threatening indeed. A fellow priest, concerned to provide opportunity for his congregation to develop such awareness, announced a period of ten minutes' silence in the context of the service of Evensong. Because there had been no previous training in centering in the heart rather than the head, near panic spread. After the service a somewhat irritated member of the congregation commented, 'What a waste of time, Vicar, we could have sung several hymns.' To which the disappointed pastor added, 'at God'!

Let us look now at the function of the Scriptures in the confirming of inner knowledge. For as we have seen, it is the crystallized form which confirms that which is perceived by the heart. This is the highest function of the Scriptures. The abuse of the Scriptures is so to use them as to feed a surfeit of religious information to the intellect on the mistaken assumption that the intellect is capable of passing this on to the heart. A recognition of this fact has an immediate significance for both the corporate and the private use of the Old and New Testaments. The former function has the effect of evoking an intuitive response of 'Yes I know' from the heart, with the corresponding developing of a true self-consciousness. The abuse of Scripture produces an assertion by the intellect that 'I am correctly informed', with a by-passing of the capacity for true understanding, a corresponding increase in religious knowledge and a growth in self-deception. When operating on the higher level the Scriptures are heard in an entirely new way, for they are heard and received with a faculty which without conscious awakening lies dormant within the human being. This faculty is that of the inner ear. It is here alone that there is an infallible recognition of the truth.

All this implies a use of Scripture fundamentally different from that in common religious practice. It is something quite other than what is commonly called Bible study. It is also different from the analysis of Scripture for the purpose of producing theological definitions, ethical systems and ecclesiastical frameworks. Nevertheless the Scriptures contain important guidelines and clues in relation to truth. What are they?

The first of these may be called the 'How of Learning'. This is exemplified *par excellence* in the ministry of Jesus. 'He taught them', says Matthew, 'many things, but without a parable taught he not' (Matt. 13.34).

Those nurtured through childhood in the catechetical tradition of the Anglican Church will recall its classic definition of a parable as 'an earthly story with a heavenly meaning'. So far so good, but by whom is the meaning known and received, and from whom is it hidden? A clue is given in the parable of the Sower. 'Those who received the word into an honest and good heart', these are capable of receiving heavenly meaning, for they have ears to hear. For the ones who are not attuned, that is whose hearts are 'waxed gross', there is an earthly story, beautifully compelling but no more than information.

To ignore this principle is to miss the first step towards the cultivation of the heart's capacity to understand; and not infrequently it gives precedence to studying and propagating the parables rather than perceiving and operating within an understanding of the parabolic principle.

William Law, the eighteenth-century English mystic, warned John Wesley, the fervent evangelist, of this very danger. He reminded him that the intellect is just as capable of playing with the excellent thoughts of 'heart warming' and 'heart conversion' as with any other ideas.

The fervent propagation of 'truth' thus becomes the great hindrance to and substitute for true learning. Indeed it makes understanding impossible, for it ignores the fundamental requirement of all who would come to a knowledge of the truth, that is the necessity for discovering first of all the 'How of Learning'. It does no more than set in motion the process concerning which the Scriptures warn us, of 'ever learning and never coming to a knowledge of the truth'. In short it is the awakening of the faculty for a true perception which must be achieved before information is made available, and such information is to be provided with very great care.

In the religious community to which I belong the Scriptures are treated with great reverence. Consequently they are used with economy. At the daily celebration of the liturgy a short passage is read conveying usually not more than one main thought. The reading is preceded by a period of silence as those present attune themselves to 'listen from the heart'. Following the Scripture reading, any who wish are free to share their response to what they hear. There is no discussion, as this inevitably smothers perception and reduces contemplative awareness to spiritually profitless analysis. After another period of silence the passage is read again.

The second New Testament principle in relation to truth is the 'How of Teaching'. The operation of this principle is demonstrated in the apparently contradictory statements made by Jesus in answer to questions concerning himself. It was never his concern to give himself a unique place in the cosmos in the thinking of those to whom he spoke. Indeed this kind of preoccupation would have been not only an irrelevance in the context of the need for openness to truth, but a barrier to understanding on the part of the hearer.

It was the undeviating concern of Jesus to be the instrument of awakening to truth as each was able to perceive it. As such his ministry was that of the perfect catalyst. Preoccupation with his person would prevent this and become intellectual speculation. This he discouraged. When there were cries of 'Blessed is the womb that bare you and the breasts that gave you suck,' he countered with 'No, rather blessed are they who hear the word of God and keep it' (Luke 11.27–8).

A great deal of theological speculation is wasted, leading only into culs-de-sac of sterile definition when we fail to perceive this. The harmonizing of the Gospels and the apparently contradictory statements of Jesus may indeed have academic and literary significance. In relation to knowledge of the truth they have no primary place. Jesus who 'knew what was in man' was aware of the level from which questions proceeded. He spoke therefore according to the level of their understanding. Information beyond the need of the present moment was not given. There was no 'casting of pearls before swine'. He knew the extent of the enquirer's capacity and answered accordingly. Contrary to the generally accepted methods of Christian evangelism, he was careful never to encourage speculation nor to present his hearers with a deposit of faith. So to the young man who calls him 'good', he replies with the question, 'Why do you call me good? There is none good but one, God' (Mark 10.18). To the disciples he says, 'You call me Master and Lord, and you say well for so I am' (John 13.13). To the man whose sight he has restored Jesus asks, 'Do you believe in the Son of Man?' and on receiving his reply accepts his worship (John 9.33–8). To Nicodemus, the trained theologian who readily acknowledged him as a teacher, Jesus exposes the division between his theologically trained mind and his lack of true knowledge by asking, 'Are you a master of Israel and know not these things?' (John 3.10). To Pilate's question, 'What is truth?' (John 18.38) Jesus did not reply, for no answer is possible!

Since the middle of the last decade there has been a significant development within the context of New Age spirituality. As we have seen, the 1960s and 1970s witnessed the great trek to the East, the search for enlightenment through the spiritual teachers and gurus of Hinduism and Buddhism. Today there is a movement from East to West. It is made up of those who, through their contact with religions other than Christianity, have become awakened to the realities I have described. Many are now returning to their own spiritual and cultural roots, searching for ways in which they can relate to Christianity. Yet it would be a mistake to see them as looking for quick incorporation into exclusive ecclesiastical frameworks, or as ready to receive package deals of doctrine and dogma. As one such seeker who had spent five years in India expressed it, 'My Indian experience has taught me how to listen and to learn from the heart. This has given me a new appreciation of the Christian Scriptures. Jesus has assumed a stature which I never dreamed of from my early experience of conventional Christianity. All this is due to my Hindu teacher. Please help me to

practise the disciplines I have learned in relation to Christianity.'

It is in the light of such a 'cry from the heart' that we must
look at what is declared to be the propagation of truth in and
through the institution of the Church today. For that which is
frequently declared to be witness to and proclamation of truth,
is seen to be no more than the impact of mind upon mind
enforced with emotional pressure. Teaching and evangelism
thus become agencies by which thought patterns are dramatically changed and intellects saturated and satisfied. So the great
religious counterfeit is established. 'The truth' takes over from
truth, and proclamation of the truth is substituted for awakening to the truth as it is in Jesus.

It was this very pattern which operated through those con-
temporaries of Jesus, the fervent propagators of religious truth
and the custodians of orthodoxy, the Pharisees. To such Jesus
spoke solemn words of warning: 'You compass sea and land to
make one proselyte and make him twofold more a child of
bondage than yourself' (Matt. 23.15).

It is from this morass of self-deception, where teaching is
equated with indoctrination and where learning has become
mere intellectual acquisitiveness, that many both inside and
outside of the Churches are seeking to extricate themselves.

8

Questions of Belief

It is now more than thirty years since the beginning of the social and religious upheavals which gave birth to the concept of a New Age. In observing the movement's evolution over these three decades it is important to keep in mind the distinction between the authentic dynamic or spiritual centre of the movement and the peripheral or cultic crystallizations, the former operating through some of its outstanding Centres, the latter increasingly apparent in the proliferation of psychic culs-de-sac. In its comparatively short span of life, Aquarius has in tones of great clarity proclaimed lofty spiritual values and powerfully demonstrated effective techniques of transformation. It is clear, however, that the former has outstripped the latter. The child of Aquarius has been clothed in magnificent robes of Light, Love and Peace. Yet there is considerable evidence to show that a strong Piscean element still operates beneath the splendid appearance. Aquarius frequently displays an appetite for the diet of its predecessor Pisces and, propelled by ideals beyond its capacity to assimilate, quietly resorts to the Piscean characteristic of egoistical power in order to attain its aims.

The passage of time has brought to light and focused the inexorable law that cult follows hard on the heels of dynamic, and that organism invariably surrenders to organization. In spite of the movement's insistence that faith is now fulfilled in knowledge, the pertinent question is, 'What kind of knowledge; that of the head or of the heart?'

What is now apparent is that where experiential wisdom ceases to be the criterion of rebirth into the age of Aquarius, then a new dogmatism arises. The pattern of this dogmatism is not difficult to discover, and at the beginning of the 1990s it is fast assuming credal shapes. How are we to assess and evaluate that development?

Evidence of its existence first appeared on the horizon of my own life in the form of a letter. 'Dear John,' it began. I was puzzled. The letter was from someone I had met on several occasions and who knew me well by name. The contents of the letter, whilst flattering my ego, left me a convinced unbeliever. The gist of the contents were as follows. The writer, who signed herself 'Mary Magdalene', had 'psychic insight into the past'. This insight had 'revealed' to her that in a previous incarnation I had been John the beloved disciple. She was Mary Magdalene! The implications of all this were that 'we had work to do together'. I had little difficulty in dismissing these fantasies as a quick path into spiritual schizophrenia and a crisis of identity. In fairness one must add that few serious exponents of reincarnation would countenance such ego-feeding imaginings. Nevertheless it has fast become a *sine qua non* that if you are truly New Age you believe in reincarnation, and for many it is the very cornerstone of Aquarian belief.

Of the five great world religions only two, Hinduism and Buddhism, teach reincarnation. But there is no simple single theory of what exactly reincarnates into matter. According to Hinduism it is the ego or indestructible self which repeatedly assumes form in this life. Buddhists have no doctrine of an individual self or ego. For them it is forms of consciousness which reincarnate, though it is left undefined as to whether the plurality of consciousnesses represented by each sentient being has any kind of separate identity.

The reality behind these theories is that consciousness in some form or other is indestructible. As in the physical world, release into higher forms is achieved by the transmuting of energy. This is the evolutionary process by which the human and the divine find union. The reverse process is conscious disintegration. Both are possible. One of the two is inevitable. Nothing remains static.

In its assertion of the indestructible nature of the soul, Christianity directs attention to the same reality but it proposes no theories of reincarnation of separate identities. At the Council of Constantinople in AD 553 reincarnation was rejected from the Church's teaching, thus leaving the message of transformation through Christ in a life span as the uniquely Christian message.

In previous ages diversity, division and separateness have been necessary in order to preserve the identities of separated cultures and societies. In the light of a contemplative philosophy we should now be able to penetrate beyond these definitions and theories which divide. To cultivate them or to seek to establish them as articles of belief is a contradiction in terms of the New Age dynamic. With the growth of a one-world consciousness it is now important to rediscover the essence of truth behind the diversity of forms. For herein lies essential unity. How is this to be done? Theories of reincarnation belong within the restrictive and limited terms of past and future. Today's movement must be from linear to penetrative thought, so to discover the meaning of the present moment. It is this activity of the human mind that is put into operation by the practice of contemplative meditation.

Hard on the heels of belief in reincarnation follows belief in vegetarianism as the hallmark of the true child of Aquarius. What are the reasons for this? There is of course the very practical and obvious fact that meat is increasingly expensive, and whereas most of our ancestors ate meat twice daily only few can afford this today. Others adopt vegetarianism because it appears to make sound economic sense. The process of growing cereals in order to feed animals could, it is argued, be profitably reduced to growing cereals in order to feed humans – full stop! Another reason for a tendency to abandon meat eating is the increasing realization amongst many caring people of the suffering caused to animals by the intensive farming methods which greed for profit has produced in Western Europe.

All such reasons are clearly commendable. There is, however, at a certain level of New Age thought, the fallacy that to eat meat is in some way less spiritual than the eating of vegetables, which in common jargon 'produce finer vibrations'!

But humanitarianism and respect for all creatures is not to be given the shape of a pseudo-spirituality. This is to invert the laws of being and of growth. It is also to misunderstand the interrelationship of all creation. To the human being it is given to transmute energy from lower to higher forms. This is done at the mental and spiritual level of our being, and also at the physical. The lower thus gives place to the higher. The truly conscious human being controls all forms of energy and is not controlled by them. This is the meaning of the words at the end of St Mark's Gospel (16.18) that 'if they drink any deadly thing it shall not hurt them'. This same truth is also expressed in the words of Jesus, 'There is nothing from without a man that entering into him can defile him; but the things which come out of him, those are they that defile the man' (Mark 7.15).

At the heart of the new creed is belief in a destiny determined by astrological influences. What is to be understood by this?

Astrology is concerned with the interaction between the elemental forces of the universe, particularly as they operate within the human psyche. Each human being contains within itself all the elements represented by the material substances of creation. The interaction between these substances is the magnetic attractions of like calling to like, which therefore encompass and influence the emotional dispositions of the human race. These influences vary according to the movements of stars and planets. Cycles with varying intensity of particular magnetism are reflected in times and places upon the earth's surface. In this way variations in manifestations are reproduced within the human race, so influencing 'natural' man, or the man of the earth.

All this has to do with natural law and natural phenomena. It is from subjection to these elemental forces and predispositions that a higher law, called by the Christian Church 'grace', operates to raise us. Grace is the divine impulse within humanity which not only counteracts all the magnetic attractions of the elemental forces, but enables the human being consciously to appropriate them as substance for what St Paul calls the 'new' or 'heavenly man' (1 Cor. 15.4). This man contains all the resources of the universal elements but is no longer controlled by them. According to the extent that a human will is allied to grace, so does that human being become a co-worker with Christ in the creation of the 'new heaven and the new earth'.

While therefore astrology gives some insight into the interrelation of all creation and the forces to be channelled and directed, full insight is given when our observation is taken from the perspective of the law of grace. I recall, during a lecture on human destiny which I had been invited to give whilst visiting New Zealand, indicating that we might profitably look at the significance of astrology. A whole row of what was later described as 'very committed Christians' rose to their feet and left the church. Sadly, it is this kind of 'commitment' which reinforces the partial understanding enshrined in the 'new creed'.

In 1969 there appeared on the market a book entitled *Testimony of Light* by Helen Greaves. The author, known to me personally, claimed that the book's contents, which consisted of descriptions of life after death, were communications from her deceased friend, Frances Banks, who during her lifetime had been a nun in the Anglican Community of the Resurrection. Helen and Frances had before the latter's death established a strong telepathic link. This link, the author maintained, was restored after Frances Banks' death. The book had instant and widespread appeal. Both the author and the communicator had been members of the recently founded Churches' Fellowship for Spiritual and Psychical Studies. Helen Greaves, a gifted and deeply spiritual woman, claimed no more than that she was a 'sensitive'. In Chapter 1, entitlted 'The Return', she describes the essence of the messages received from Frances as concerned with 'a oneness with the Divine Company of Heaven, resulting in a new intuitive perception of unity and inspiration for radiant living'. 'This', writes the author, 'is what Frances Banks felt to be the message for the New Age into which we are now emerging, a greater extension of man's consciousness, so that even during the limitation of earthly life he can enter the beauty of the spiritual worlds and receive inspiration therefrom.'

It is this modern interpretation of what constitutes a kind of Communion of Saints that has been firmly woven into a new belief pattern. Since the publication of *Testimony of Light* many such books have appeared, purporting to relay teachings from the next life. In most instances the authors make claim to the word 'sensitive' rather than 'spiritualist'. For some reason, not entirely clear, the former description is thought to describe a higher level of communication between the living and the dead. The 'communicator' is usually claimed to be a very 'highly evolved soul'.

The Church has frequently pronounced anathemas on attempts to communicate with the dead. In the context of today's spiritual search such condemnations count for very little. The question which must be asked, however, is whether such communications aid growth into maturity in this life. All valid aids, whether from the physical sphere or from any other, throw us back upon our own potential. True teachers, whether from this place or from another, will never create a dependence complex. Rather they will enable the seeker to discover and relate to his own true self. If such communication with the departed does this, then it may be seen to be an aspect of Christian belief in the Communion of Saints.

Closely allied to this intercommunion is belief in spiritual gifts. The gifts sought after bear a remarkable parallel to those experienced in Charismatic renewal circles. The prevalence of healing we have already examined. To this we may add clairvoyance, discernment of spirits, tongues and their interpretation. Frequently these gifts appear when there is an experience of release from conventional stereotyped behaviour patterns into a free expression of the emotions.

From my observation of New Age Centres where this occurs, the acquisition of these psychic gifts, described by St Paul in 1 Corinthians chapter 12, commonly breeds a sense of superiority and power, added to which may be claims to a superior belief pattern. Sadly, there is often ignorance of St Paul's commendation of the 'more excellent way', the way of *agape*, described in chapter 13.

The apocalyptic note sounded in the Christian creed has its counterpart in a great variety of beliefs concerning changes which are expected to take place in the planet before the end of this century. These vary from expectation that the ancient mythical city of Atlantis will, as a result of earthquakes, rise again from the depths of the ocean, to a belief that large parts of the earth's surface will disintegrate and disappear. Allied to this is the expectation of the 'world teacher'. Already we have referred to the influence of Alice Bailey and Rudolf Steiner on New Age thinking. The former produced a book, allegedly containing communications from a departed saint called D.K., entitled *The Reappearance of the Christ*. The latter, writing from his own understanding, described this mystery as 'the true nature of the Second Coming'.

The mystery is to be seen as comprehending creation in all its aspects and dimensions. It is necessary therefore to understand that the planet to which the human race is substantially related has more than one face. According to the New Testament, the physical aspect of the world is but a manifestation in time and space of a greater reality to which in the fullness of time it must yield itself up.

The planet has evolved from earlier forms of manifestation and the process of evolution continues. Two governing principles are to be observed: (a) that nothing in the universe of matter is static, and (b) that the material universe is like the definition of a Christian sacrament, 'an outward and visible sign of an inward and spiritual grace'. A third factor to be understood is that humanity itself is part of the changes which underlie and penetrate all matter. A true self-consciousness therefore gives insight into and understanding of the nature of the changes which are already taking place and prompts an awakening into further understanding.

The end of a world is not to be looked for primarily by physical changes effected from without but rather by an eruption of life from within. This has the twofold aspect of a leap from the imprisonment of the time-space continuum, when for those with eyes to see a new aspect of the Christ who 'fills all things' bursts into manifestation.

9

The New Contemplatives

Early in 1988 I received an invitation from the secretary of an organization based on the outskirts of Chichester in Sussex. 'As you will probably know,' ran the letter, 'we are an independent New Age Group representing people on a spiritual path from a great variety of backgrounds. Would you please come and address us on a subject of your choice and offer us a date about a year from now.'

The phrase 'on a spiritual path' had begun to have a familiar ring. It was part of the vocabulary of the new world within which I was learning to move with increasing ease, and I recognized it as describing 'experiential wisdom'.

Replying in the same coded language I said that I would be very happy to come and suggested as the title of my lecture 'The New Contemplatives'. Already I had discovered that 'contemplative' was a word which had crossed over the ecclesiastical boundaries and was now happily lodged in the New Age vocabulary.

Back came the reply: 'This is exactly the sort of thing we are looking for.' On my way to Chichester the following October I was still pondering the problem of language. Were we, I wondered, talking about the same thing? By the time the evening session had ended I had no doubt that we were.

The format for the evening was fairly traditional: lecture, half-an-hour's break for refreshments and informal chatting, questions, followed by closing meditation. During the break I took the opportunity to discover as much as I could about the

150 or so people present. By now I was well used to the term
'great diversity' being used to describe such gatherings. It was
certainly true on this occasion. A delightful Jewish lady whom
I had observed listening very intently during the address posed
a theologically intriguing question. In my address I had spoken
of the New Testament experience of the 'indwelling Christ',
described by many mystics as the 'I Am consciousness'. 'I have
been on a spiritual path for a number of years,' she told me,
'and although you are using Christian terminology to describe
this reality and my roots are in the Old Testament, is it not
possible that I as a Jewess may speak of this experience as
identical with my deep awareness of Yahweh or "I Am"?' I
had no doubt that it was.

Most of the young people present had no religious connec-
tions. They were warmly responsive to what they conceived to
be the 'essence' of the message, though they confessed themselves rather 'foxed' with some of my strange vocabulary! They
also queried why it was necessary to use religious language at all
for what was clearly to do with Huxley's 'Perennial Philosophy'.
'But', said one of them, 'we have to learn not to equate the
reality of a thing with the language which we use to convey it.'
I was reminded of the comment of a brother priest who had
accompanied me on a visit to one of the Centres: 'As one
long used to the protection given by theological and religious
language, I felt stripped of all possibility of pretence when it
was taken from me!'

As far as the Church was concerned, the young had little or
no knowledge of it. They had never had direct contact with the
Church. They saw it as an ancient institution worthy of respect
which had historically played an important part in the formation
of the nation. In the 'Piscean Age' it had provided society and
individuals with the necessary structures and laws. Beyond that
they were agnostic. It had, they volunteered, produced very
great mystics, but they could see no contemporary connection
between it and the spiritual path today. Nevertheless, they
were clearly intrigued that now one of its professionals, who

had introduced himself as 'totally orthodox', should as they put it 'be able to tune into this wavelength'. They were, however, responsive to the philosophy of the contemplative Order which I represented, that there is no conflict between 'experiential wisdom' and orthodox doctrine, and that they are simply different levels of understanding.

About half a dozen participants, all middle-aged, introduced themselves as members of a meditation group which met every week in a village school about ten miles away. All of them had roots in the Church, and for them the occasion was an affirming one. They had been drawn together by a common desire to practise the presence of God. They had 'longed for silence' and whilst they were loyal members of the Church they longed for opportunities to be still and listen instead of, as one of them graphically put it, 'filling up all the spaces in worship by singing hymns and listening to so many Bible readings'. They explained that they were a completely open group and that the only qualification for joining was a desire to 'learn how to centre in the heart'. 'We know what it is that joins us together but we find it difficult to explain what we know. This evening has put our common experience into words.'

There were, of course, some at the gathering who had felt hurt or rejected by the Church; who, wanting to share their experience with the clergy, had been rebuffed with accusations of 'dabbling in the occult'.

An enthusiastic retired army officer and his wife informed me that they never missed these monthly meetings. 'You see, they feed us spiritually and we meet with fellow travellers on the way. On Sundays we worship at the Cathedral and since coming here we find that it means so much more to us.'

On the literature table there was ample evidence of the broad spectrum of interest represented in such groups: *The Meaning of Ley Lines*, *The Gnostic Gospels*, *The Aquarian Gospel of Jesus Christ*, *What is a Sensitive?*, *The Ancient Wisdom*, and a plethora of healing literature. There were also books to reassure the orthodox: Cardinal Hume on spirituality and books on the Christian mystics.

Question time brought forth the questions with which I was now becoming quite familiar. Did I, as an Anglican priest, not find the Church difficult to cope with? 'No more', I replied, 'then do all my brother clergy.' How did I square my commitment to orthodoxy with an obvious recognition of the validity of the path of the mystic? The answer to this, I assured them, could be found in the writings available on the bookstall: St John of the Cross, Meister Eckhart, Hildegard of Bingen and many more. And what about doctrine and dogma? These, we agreed, were all the crystallizations in static form of a powerful dynamic, and properly understood there is no contradiction. Curiosity satisfied, the evening reached its conclusion with a led meditation.

I departed with the strong impression, so often experienced in my contact with such groups, that here in the context of avid enquiry and a bewildering array of possible paths were many who had a deep understanding of that which Jesus described as 'entering in through the strait gate', and were in truth travelling along a contemplative path.

What then is this path, and what are the criteria by which its validity is to be judged? Before considering this we need first to be clear as to what contemplation is not. It has nothing to do with what is commonly called clairvoyance. The clairvoyant penetrates into that psychic world which, as we have seen, is created by the whole range of human emotions, a world which has no ultimate significance. It is the world of visions, ecstasies and alleged communications with the departed.

Contemplation, as we saw in Chapter Four, is to do with a way of seeing which is basic to the teachings of the New Testament. Its effects are to go beyond appearances and to touch reality by another mode of operation. It is that capacity for seeing of which Jesus declared the pharisaical or conditioned mind to be incapable. 'You have eyes', Jesus declared, 'and you see not, ears and you hear not, neither do you understand'

(Mark 8.18). This seeing, according to the New Testament, is not the prerogative of an élitist or specialist religious group; rather it is central to a realization of the gospel in its fullness.

All the 'People of the Way', as the early Christians were known, must by their very awakenedness in Christ participate in some measure in this seeing. To those whose seeing and perceptions were confined to the visible, albeit religious world, Jesus said, 'Stop judging by appearances and make a right judgement' (John 7.24). The Messianic utterances of Isaiah declared that 'He will not judge by what he sees with his eyes, nor decide what he hears by his ears' (Isa. 11.3). In what have been called the two 'cosmic Epistles', those to the Ephesians and the Colossians, St Paul expressed the prayer that 'the eyes of your heart may be opened, that you may KNOW . . . ' (Eph. 1.18; cf. Col. 2.2,3). This seeing with the eyes of the heart becomes in the New Testament a mode of 'being in the world but not of it', that is, not limited by sense perception, not motivated by, nor enmeshed in, the cul-de-sac which determines the limitations of what St Paul described as 'the natural man'.

The contemplative path, then, is the way of Christocentric awakening, for it is concerned with 'heart wisdom'.

During my examination of the bookstall I came across a number of copies of the book *The Way of the Pilgrim*, and its sequel *The Pilgrim Continues His Way*. Observing my interest, the lady in charge of the stall commented, 'That is a very popular book amongst the young people. It is a presentation of Jesus Christ to which they can respond immediately.'

The theme of the book is the use of the Jesus Prayer for the awakening of the heart. The prayer in its full form, 'Lord Jesus Christ, Son of God, have mercy upon me, a sinner', has a long history in the Orthodox churches of the East. At first the whole sentence is repeated with great concentration. Gradually, as awareness becomes centred in the heart, the prayer is verbally reduced until only the word 'Jesus' is repeated over and over again. Finally, all words are relinquished and consciousness is focused within the still centre of the heart. The movement is one of step-by-step progression from a devotion to Jesus to the indwelling Christ.

It is important to remember that the prayer is not a magic formula having automatic effects. It is a particular technique which, with the right motivation, may be a powerful means to awaken the heart to 'the truth as it is in Jesus'. The same effects may be achieved by any systematic, correctly motivated, steps which lead beyond mental images and words to the still centre within the depths of our being.

This path, as we have indicated, may accurately be described as that of 'mystical cognition' or 'awakening'. For experientially the mystic and the contemplative are one. Both are deeply conscious that dualism, with its separating of mind and matter, physical and spiritual, belongs to the world of sense perception, and that beyond all this is a world where in some mysterious way, the observed and the observer are one.

The functions of what I have described as the 'new contemplatives' differ from those of the traditional concept of the mystic. The latter is characterized by an intense awareness of the unity of all things in Christ. The contemplative is concerned consciously to relate this awareness to a philosophy which embraces all life. To travel along this path is to open up ever-widening vistas of understanding and perception. This understanding manifests itself in varying degrees of intensity to different individuals. It is a perception which ranges from a clear seeing of people and their true essence to a knowledge of the reality behind all life forms. It perceives, in the words of John Donne, that 'no man is an island', and that the unitive force which holds together all creation is not an impersonal energy but that of love.

In our day a remarkable confirmation of the contemplative's perception is emerging from the world of physics. It first began to emerge in the Western world when in 1905 Albert Einstein propounded his theory of relativity, which was to lead physics to abandon forever the Newtonian theory of absolute time and absolute space. Inherent in Einstein's thinking was the conviction that space, time and the laws of motion can be defined only in reference to the condition of the observer. Suddenly the scientific observer had become like the mystic or the contemplative, part of the world which was being observed. No longer could the scientist consider himself to be a detached observer. He himself had become part of the world of physics.

In *The Story of Science*, published in 1984, this leap in scientific understanding is described by the authors Robert Augros and George Stanciu. They quote the physicist, Max Born: 'No description of any natural phenomenon in the atomic domain is possible without reference to the observer.' The authors then go on to say, 'The choice one makes about what one observes makes an irretrievable difference in what one finds. The observer is elevated from observer to participant, and in some strange way this is a participatory universe.' Such a statement can find only one response from the mystic or contemplative: 'Yes, I know.'

In April 1990, the Wrekin Trust, the convenors of the Iona conference I had attended in 1972, organized its thirteenth annual Mystics and Scientists conference in London. The conference title was 'The Nature of the Self, Psyche, Brain and Consciousness'. It is indicative of today's interest in the convergence of the spiritual and the scientific that as always it was fully subscribed long beforehand. It is also significant that this important event derived its impetus and inspiration from a New Age impulse. Yet who could doubt that those interested, mostly dissociated from organized religion, were People of the Way?

Convergence there undoubtedly is; yet discernment requires that we distinguish between the discoveries of science and those of the contemplative, a distinction not always realized in the context of New Age explorations. The new physics is now indicating the relativity of time and space, and bringing us to new vistas of reality which take us beyond both. Further scientific progress may bring us to hitherto undreamed-of revelation. The recognition of the essential links between the observer and the observed is now an indication that consciousness both pervades and extends beyond matter, thus bringing the concept of mind within scientific cognition. Yet it is only that consciousness which proceeds from human 'heart centredness' which can respond and relate to the ultimate reality we call God, and all that is packed into that word.

No scientific investigation or progress can give birth to this level of understanding. For extension of human consciousness into the 'beyond', or the establishment of a rapport with new dimensions beyond the physical, may well prove to be no more than a refined form of scientific materialism belonging to the realm of extra-sensory perception. Science is properly concerned with the fact, not the quality, of being. Its extending frontiers remain at the level of, and are determined by, its own preconceptions and the level of the scientist's own being. Like always calls to like, and only that which issues from quality of being can uncover and discover its own counterpart.

Today the exclusive assumptions of both religious and scientific methods in the West are being questioned side by side. By many, the new-style mystic and the new scientist are seen to be moving on paths of convergence. A new philosophy of life is being shaped, of which they are both an essential part.

It is sometimes asserted that those who follow the contemplative path are engaged in retreat from the harsh realities of everyday modern life. Nothing could be further from the truth. The true contemplative pursues a path of scientific enquiry which embraces the whole of life and constitutes a philosophy of wholeness. For by this path his understanding of the whole of life and the whole creation is informed. The contemplative awareness knows no dichotomy between the development of spirituality and a true social consciousness, between contemplation and a passionate concern for the planet. Indeed, the contemplative prayer life brings human beings, in the words of Teilhard de Chardin, 'to the very heart of the universe where its secrets are revealed'.

This, then, is the path along which many people from a great variety of backgrounds are now moving. It is the place of powerful convergence for many paths which lead through and from great differences in terms of belief. This is the movement of a powerful dynamic to be observed in the Western world at the end of the twentieth century.

10

What of Prayer?

'We do not, according to your Church's understanding, pray, but we do seek from the heart to align ourselves consciously to cosmic forces.' The speaker was the focalizer of a group which met regularly for meditation, and we were discussing the nature of prayer.

The statement 'according to your Church's understanding' caused me some heart searching. What exactly was this understanding? I could of course have looked up the text books, and reminded myself of the great classical definitions. But somehow none of them sounded very relevant; not because they were untrue but because they seemed strangely divorced from that experiential wisdom which undoubtedly had a prayerful content.

Many today have difficulties with the traditional definitions of prayer, yet give expression by their very being to a real prayer life. The concept of a God apart from and external to the created order, influenced to intervene in world affairs by competing pressure groups, is rejected by an increasing number of thinking and praying people. A tribal God fits uncomfortably into a one-world consciousness.

The very phrase, 'Let us pray', as reiterated in the worship of the Churches, has powerful overtones suggesting the total abasement of the creature in the presence of the Creator (a very different thing from a sense of the 'awfulness' of God). And in spite of the liturgical movement many corporate expressions of prayer still strongly imply that its effectiveness is born from endless reiterations of human worthlessness in the presence of divine perfection. This of course is a fallacy, for although such self-abnegation frequently goes hand-in-hand with protestations of belief in divine forgiveness, the sense of a great divide is only reinforced by this kind of praying. Professions of faith do nothing to effect receptivity either to forgiveness or anything else from God. So what is misnamed prayer becomes a persistent reinforcement of self-erected barriers, and the problem becomes compounded. Expectations slowly evaporate, the will becomes paralysed and the reality of an ever-present compassionate Deity is shrouded from consciousness.

So, in the context of a meaning and purpose for all creation, a meaning and purpose which endeavours to encompass our individual lives and which is shaping our consciousness, what is the essence of prayer as distinct from the watertight compartments into which we have attempted to lock it? It is fully in accord with the teaching and example of Jesus to assert that prayer is the will to align one's energies with the divine plan and purpose and to do so with disregard for outcome or personal cost. We may take this a stage further. Wherever human beings move away from introverted self-concern and give themselves to a greater good, here true prayer is being offered. This is described by Jesus in St John's Gospel (chapter 15) as the branch abiding in the vine. 'When you do this', he says, 'you shall ask what you will and it shall be done unto you' (v. 7). Once the human will is at one with the cosmic will, all things are possible, for a higher law than that of sin and death comes into play.

Such prayer is undifferentiating; that is, it will not be an expression of personal preferences or dispositions but according to the will of God. So does our praying express that of the Cosmic Being himself, uttered in the Garden of Gethsemane: 'Father, thy will, not mine, be done.'

To pray in this manner is to take into our very being the redemptive activity of God. Through the power of Holy Spirit we are becoming Christ in the world. Prayer thus ceases to be a self-centred tool by which we attempt to manipulate God but a conscious entering into a cosmic unveiling. For prayer does not change the divine will. Rather it releases it, and with this release comes first the emergence of pattern in an individual life, then its larger shape. I quote from 'The Omega Vision' in my book *The End of an Age*:

> The measure of the pattern's growing and its fast becoming
> Are all determined by a Master Weaver,
> And yet the Master does not weave alone;
> For all are masters who in that shape are weaving.
> The threads, the colours and the constitution of its myriad
>   parts
> Are those, who being many now are one.
> And in this willing giving to the whole
> Is comprehended all communion that is holy.
> It is the yielding of the one to all, the all to One,
> The laying down and finding of a life.

Let us approach this from an even larger perspective: The parameters or twin pillars of the divine activity are those of creation and evolution. The act of creation, portrayed in poetic form in the book of Genesis, may be seen as a vast explosion of energy manifesting in time and space as matter. The eternal Source is that to which we give the name God. This Source is not to be thought of as detached from that which proceeds from it. In the first chapter of St John's Gospel, that which proceeds from the Source is described as the Word. In Christian theological terms this is the Second Person of the Trinity. God is therefore seen to be inherent within the world of matter as the Sustainer. The stream of energy expanding outwards from the Source also gives birth to a life force seeking to draw the essence of all created forms back to the Source itself – the Holy Spirit. The former is the process of creation, the latter that of evolution.

The world of matter thus becomes the means by which the

divine life seeks to express itself, first through multiplicity of form, then by drawing all together into the One.

This two-fold action involving expression and direction is effected only through struggle and suffering. For every form of matter contains not only potential for union with the whole and with the Source, but also the capacity for a kind of completion within itself – a circle of existence separate from the whole and therefore of only temporal duration. Such an isolated circle of existence becomes in effect a short circuit, an individualization which rejects its part within the whole. This we may see as the will of the human ego.

It is this will and capacity for self-destruction that the divine love is ever seeking to nullify. Identifying itself with all forms and manifestations, it seeks to lift all into oneness. So does a circle of limited existence become a spiral of eternal life. Through life, death and resurrection, as personified in Jesus Christ, 'life and immortality are brought to Light' – to quote St Paul's words to Timothy (2 Tim. 1.10).

The spearhead of the movement to integrate with the whole is created and operated by awakened human beings. They are awakened because they are aware of a life impulse striving to become active in and through them. They have awakened to the reality of a powerful regenerative force, personal yet all-embracing. With this they have freely chosen to co-operate. They become men and women of prayer. Or, expressed in a different framework of thought, they are aligned from the heart to cosmic forces.

Expressed in another way, it is as if all the ingredients or essential parts of a divine plan embracing time and space and all that is contained therein, are embodied within the created order, but that without a conscious 'yes' from the heart of humanity, the myriad parts cannot coalesce or come together – the shape of the whole cannot emerge. It is this 'yes' from the human heart that constitutes the essence of true prayer. Without this co-operation the impulse towards cohesion and meaning is able to do no more than pulsate within confined spheres; each level of consciousness within creation, from mineral to human, remains a world turned in upon itself, effecting no more than the completion of a physical life span.

Such an understanding of prayer gives meaning and purpose to all life. It does no violence to the intellect and is in accordance with the scientific recognition of all matter as a manifestation of energy.

All this may be seen as powerfully symbolized in the story of the appearance of the angel Gabriel to Mary. For Mary is presented with the privilege and opportunity of enabling by her wholehearted acquiescence the coming together of humanity and divinity in perfect harmony. Her 'yes' made possible the release of an impulse from the divine Source which gave birth to the Christ child. With the words 'Be it unto me according to thy word,' the birth of Jesus Christ was made possible. When creation, through a willing humanity, has sounded with a full sufficiency the prayer of 'Yes, Lord', then will Christ be manifested in his cosmic body.

The object of prayer is the realization of a unity not only within oneself, but with the divine Source and with all creation. Simplicity is the key which opens the door to a prayer-filled life, yet the vision which then unfolds is one of ever-widening vistas of perception. It is then that the great definitions of the Christian faith are recognized as confirmation of this understanding; indeed they are seen to be perfect articulations of experiential wisdom. The 'fall' is seen to be the individualizing of life, and 'original sin' the tendency to separation and isolation. The 'Holy Spirit' is recognized as the pure life force 'proceeding from the Father'. 'Incarnation' expresses the manifesting of Deity through matter, perfectly exemplified in Jesus Christ. The 'redeeming work of Christ' is identified as a perfected human will powerfully drawing humanity back into union with the Source; and to 'pray in Christ's name' as sharing in his consciousness.

11

Christ-centred Spirituality

At the age of seventeen I was 'converted'. Looking back from the perspective of forty years later, it is not easy to assess the full significance of what happened. Yet I can still recall the intensity of emotions which accompanied that 'turning to Christ'. Clearly, two important things did happen. They were important in terms of the spiritual pathway that I was to follow and of the direction it was to take. For two processes, eventually to become uncomfortable bedfellows and then incompatible, were dramatically and simultaneously brought to birth.

The first of these processes was a commitment to a new and unfolding world of spiritual values. This was a world full of beckoning promise and potential. The second was the experience of being catapulted into the powerful and encapsulating world of religious dogma. I was entering a thought structure consisting of absolute certainties concerning the nature of God, humanity and the universe.

The first process was soon to require a continuous readjustment of thinking, to ensure submission to this world of absolutes. And for many years the second process was to control and direct the course of the first. The result was the systematic shaping of an enquiring mind into an unquestioning conformity. It was years later that I was to discover for myself the essential difference between the two processes and to allow the first that freedom which is of the very substance of true spiritual awakening.

What is the nature of this awakening, and how does it relate to those spiritual impulses which we have been examining? In attempting to answer the first part of this question we are confronted immediately with difficulty. For spiritual awakening is response to the action of a movement or dynamic (that is, the divine dynamic operating both within the human psyche and in human affairs), and a dynamic by its very nature defies and eludes definition. To attempt therefore to seal its meaning within a dogmatic formula is a contradiction in terms.

This movement is capable of a multitude of expressions and its modes of operation are beyond calculation. It cannot be trapped or held within any one category of manifestation. To attempt to do so is in effect to obscure those realities towards which it points and to which it gives authentic expression. It is to impose limits on the limitless.

Further, this movement cannot be determined or judged by any static form of identification any more than the sun can be equated with one of its myriad rays. It is authenticated only by itself; for it is 'the truth' which, says Jesus, 'shall set you free' (John 8.32). Like the nature of truth, spiritual awakening is primarily concerned not with intellectual concepts but with the reality of a situation – every situation. Operating as the spear-head of a struggle between human egocentricity and divisiveness on the one hand and the divine principle of wholeness on the other, it may be recognized within infinite diversity and behind any one of a thousand forms.

Spirituality eludes not only definitions but also the natural processes of comprehension. It cannot be grasped by the intellect, for linear thinking can never comprehend the spiritual. Access to the world of spiritual reality is by the way of contradiction and paradox. As the apostle Paul stated so unequivocally, 'The natural man [the sense-bound] does not understand the things of God, for they are spiritually discerned' (1 Cor. 2.14). Such discernment comes through the operation of penetrative or intuitive thought, and this emerges from the point where opposites come together. The intellectual processes, having reached an impasse, allow themselves to become stilled.

This produces the focusing of a new perception; for the mind, like a still, clear pool, then begins to reflect reality. So does spiritual discernment come to birth, and the contemplative path unfold.

Such discernment constitutes an immediate recognition of the validity of paradox and the significance of apparent opposites. For it knows that, although those human faculties which operate only in time and space can never themselves perceive the spiritual, yet it is through these very faculties that the dynamic is ever being articulated within human affairs. Proceeding from the world of ultimate reality (the spiritual world), it is ever working within these dimensions to illuminate and reconcile. Never stilled, this most powerful of all movements makes its presence known within human consciousness, and human beings are the prisms through which its myriad facets are focused on the planet. While speaking with a multitude of voices, the single word 'love' may give it perfect utterance, and it is heard best of all in the silence of the heart.

All this was perfectly illustrated by Jesus when he pointed Nicodemus towards the necessity of new birth. 'Those who are born of the spirit', he declared, 'are like the wind. No one knows from where it comes or where it goes, for it blows where it will' (John 3.8). The essence of spiritual awakening then may be summed up as follows:

> It is the space to see, to be, to move
> and quickly to outgrow those limitations
> which the pattern of our living has imposed upon us.
>
> (The Omega Vision)

Such an understanding makes it clear that the dynamic of the spiritual man can never be identified with credal statements, however perfectly expressed. Nor can it be contained within a catechism, however excellent its precepts. It is equally true that both creed and catechism, in particular situations and places, may give it perfect expression and articulation. For as we have seen, between movement and static form there need be no contradiction; a differentiation perceived by the mystics of all ages.

Where, then, is the point of beginning for conscious awakening to this spiritual dimension? All of us must begin from exactly where we are and from within the context of our present understanding. Beliefs as such play no necessary part in such a beginning. Conversely, agnosticism provides no valid excuse for lack of response. Response to what? All that is necessary for movement toward human fulfilment and humanity's true destiny is a readiness to respond to the beckoning of the highest that we know. It may be that we shall quickly find that the highest has become inadequate. No matter, for it will take us beyond itself to ever-widening vistas waiting to unfold within our consciousness. This is the nature of conversion and the essence of new birth.

Is a conscious faith in God not then a necessary prerequisite for the beginning of each unfolding? To this the answer must be 'no'. If the desire for change, growth, fulfilment, whatever we may choose to call it, is there, then this is a clear indication that there is already an awakening from within, and what we call 'God' is undoubtedly the initiator of the process.

The word 'God' represents that reality which may emerge under many names or none. Recognition of the reality may well lead to a clear expression of belief in God, but this plays no necessary part in spiritual awakening. Indeed there are concepts of God which may inhibit or hinder the development of what in fact is a God-centred evolution of life from within, an aligning of the will with the dynamic. Movement with integrity contains the essence of belief, and reaching towards the highest that we know constitutes the advent of what the theologians call 'saving faith'. Yet names and titles, theological or otherwise, have only secondary significance.

The authentic face of God is love. It was this which drew seekers after the dynamic so powerfully to Jesus of Nazareth. Their experience of his undifferentiating self-giving led them to declare, 'We have seen the glory of God in the face of Jesus Christ' (cf. 2 Cor. 4.6).

Many of us have unconsciously inherited images of a God who is 'out there' and apart from the whole of creation. Yet the primary manifestation of divinity as divine love is in and through the created order. This is beautifully expressed in what is sometimes called the Prologue of St John's Gospel (1.1–14). Here the whole universe is seen to be the outward vesture of a veiled but revealed divinity, or what has been called in the Christian tradition the Cosmic Christ. It is an awareness of this which characterizes the spiritual consciousness rising within Western society today.

The maelstrom of change which we have examined has in many areas now subsided, and as we enter the last decade of the century there are indications within society of frantic attempts to rebuild the contours of a rapidly disappearing world. The absence of the old sources of authority and the threat of global destruction are producing an unrelenting pressure upon human consciousness. In this context we are confronted with the choice of trying to re-establish the old or to move forward with the dynamic into a world of new realities. What are the signs of hope for the future?

Beneath the diversity of interpretations and the sometimes chaotic residue of past patterns of thought and behaviour, creative new impulses are emerging. And these are refusing to operate within the confines of those separate compartments which have for so long divided humanity. The old structures of thought provided by religion, philosophy and science cease to have meaning for human beings who are striving to align themselves with these new impulses. The old skins cannot contain the new wine. It is to this that the New Age bears witness.

A new and universal self-awareness is struggling to be born. Its distinctive characteristic is a realization of a unity which, existing already at a deeper level, is now seeking to manifest at all levels of society. This deep urge towards unity permeates every aspect of human endeavour and creativity. That attempts to realize it at the level of politics, economics and religion repeatedly founder on the still powerful rocks of a divisive egocentricity checks, but does not extinguish, the movement. For this is more than a vague outreach towards the unknown and the unattainable. It is the expression of life welling up from within the human psyche itself, the release of a new creative energy which is at the heart of all true spiritual awakening.

The search and the yearning have many faces. Yet all are part of a convergence, the significance of which has yet to be realized; but the time is surely ripe to give meaning, purpose and a sense of direction to what is happening. This can only be done by those who are prepared to go the way of conscious co-operation.

Central to what is happening is a growing recognition of an essential link between the human race, all sentient beings and the planet itself. The interdependence of all life is now beyond question. The recognition of this ranges from the ecologically concerned to the mystically aware. Indeed these two frequently appear as complementary aspects or facets of a single perception, which is that all physical manifestations of life relate to a planetary significance which goes beyond the physical.

The meaning of this eruption into universal consciousness cannot be over-emphasized. Indeed its implications are enormous. For it signifies the disappearance of the old dichotomy between the material and the spiritual. This old dichotomy, so long reinforced by both science and religion, is no longer tenable.

For those with eyes to see and ears to hear, it is possible to see in the events of Christ's life, death and resurrection mirror images reflecting the spiritual impulses which are endeavouring to bring humanity a stage further in its search for union with the Source. In the historical image presented by the incarnation of Christ there is mirrored the unity of the earthly and the heavenly, a confirmation of what is now breaking into universal consciousness. For what is now happening is a cosmic re-enactment of the birth of the child in Bethlehem. It is the Christ who is struggling to come to birth. The process is one of struggle, for it is taking place in a universe where manifestly there is disharmony, disintegration and conflict. The struggle is towards and for the harmonizing of the universe, that is, of universal harmony. The end of the evolutionary process will be the perfect manifestation of the Divine Principle, or the revealing of the whole Christ in and through the cosmos; the harmonizing of all things – or in specifically Christian terminology, the Second Coming or *Parousia*.

The spearhead of the struggle, as we saw in the previous chapter, is manifest within the human kingdom. It is a struggle between human egocentricity and divisiveness on the one hand, and the Divine Principle which creates wholeness on the other. Whenever in the history of humanity individuals or groups have through suffering and struggle, that is, through the way of the cross, aligned themselves with the evolutionary thrust, there facets of true humanity have broken through and the Christ Spirit has been incarnated.

Within Jesus we may see a complete aligning of the human individuality or ego with this Divine Principle. In such an incarnation we see a whole person perfectly harmonized within and with the created order. With a true self-consciousness, which was at the same time a cosmic consciousness, Jesus was therefore able to say, 'I am the way, the truth and the life.' Here was a prototype of what human beings are destined to be. In him a 'Christed humanity' was manifested, a declaration of what it is to be truly human.

It follows from this, I believe, that to ally oneself consciously with the Divine Principle is to be moving, in the language of the New Testament, 'in Christ, through Christ and with Christ'. It is in some measure to be a 'partaker of the divine nature' (2 Pet. 1.4), and to know something of the experience of 'Christ in me, the hope of glory' (Col. 1.27).

12

A Creation Spirituality

In the mid-1970s I was introduced to a very unusual elderly man described as 'the doyen of the New Age movement'. Rock Ogilvie Crombie was by training a scientist. Yet clearly he was much more, and I was fascinated as he shared with me some of his extraordinary experiences. His choice of language revealed a careful, probing mind. The subjects he described were those of the visionary. To hear this apparently canny Scot speak of his encounters with the god Pan as he walked along Princes Street, Edinburgh, was for me at that time to be brought to the limits of credulity. Yet here was no duplicity and no attempt to convince his hearers. He spoke of elves, sprites and many other entities from the world of nature, unemotionally and in the measured tones of the analytical chemist. For me he personified two levels of investigation into the world of nature which have gathered momentum since the 1960s, the scientific and the psychic. The former had been concerned with the measuring of consciousness within the animal and vegetable kingdom. This has on the whole proved inconclusive, providing little more than fascinating theories. The latter we need to examine a little more closely, for it has provided for many disappointing culs-de-sac leading to confusion.

Psychic investigations operate from the instinctual level of the investigator. Images and shapes which belong to the racial memory are uncovered within the human psyche. These then clothe the energies encountered by such probings. The shapes and images rise from the vast storehouse of human folklore carried by the human race from its primitive beginnings. Drawn from the deep subconscious, they belong to an earlier stage of evolution and are frequently linked to a fear of the elemental forces of nature by which primitive human beings were controlled and dominated. This is sometimes quite wrongly described as Nature Mysticism.

These elemental forces are today, in certain circles, given the currently fashionable title of '*devas*', the Hindi word for a god. What is often not realized by those who carry out these incursions into the lower kingdoms, is that to concede to these forces god-like qualities is to reinvest them with an authority which they once possessed when human beings were in bondage to them. Indeed such uncovering of the lower worlds, while sometimes surrounded with an aura of romanticism, is nothing less than a regression to an earlier stage of evolution, a path leading back into the bondage of fear. This subjection to the elemental forces is described by St Paul in his letter to the Christians at Colossae: 'Be on your guard, do not let your mind be captured by delusive speculations centred on the elemental spirits of the world . . . ' (Col. 2.8).

How then are we to understand a proper and developing relationship with the mystery of planet Earth, and how to pursue it?

Our point of beginning must be the cultivation of the kind of knowing which we have described as contemplative awareness, which carries perception beyond the visible creation to that greater reality of which it is an outward and visible sign. It is that knowing from the heart which St Paul, in his letter to the Ephesians, sets in the context of a great cosmic vision of the universe when everything in heaven and earth is to be brought into a unity.

Here is no fanciful speculation or self-delusion for, as the quiet mind or the still, clear pool of reflection is created within, we begin to move from the world of the apparent to the real. To this mode of seeing, the four kingdoms of creation – animal, human, vegetable and mineral – are seen not as by the physical eye, separate the one from the other, but interrelated and all contributing to a harmonious and evolving pattern.

Beneath the human and the animal kingdom are those of the vegetable and the mineral upon which both depend. Man's rapacious plundering of the earth's resources during the past century has highlighted this dependance as never before. Without the life they surrender to the human being, humanity cannot continue to exist.

Within the total make-up of the human are contained all the energies of the lower kingdoms, animal, vegetable and mineral. To man is given to behold this vast potential within himself and to lay hold consciously upon the unlimited resources which rise within him from these lower levels, and from them fashion the pattern of what the New Testament calls the 'new man in Christ'. 'For this,' says St Paul in the Epistle to the Romans, 'the whole creation is groaning and travailing, waiting for the manifestation of the children of God.'

This process is reflected and symbolized at the physical level. It is perhaps most clearly seen in the relationship between the kingdoms. We may observe this in three areas: firstly in the powers of the animal kingdom, controlled, tamed and utilized by the human. Secondly in a unique relationship of harmony which has developed over the centuries as man has domesticated many of the species. Thirdly as the animal provides for the human being a source of food by which the physical being is sustained. Each of these three areas mirrors and symbolizes a larger significance.

In the non-physical world there is immediate connection between the animal and the human. This functions in the world of appetite and desire. Here separation and isolation do not exist as in the physical world. The whole range of the lower emotions exists as a commonality between the two. That dimension of humanity commonly called the animal nature co-exists with and interpenetrates that of the animal kingdom. There are no separate containers such as exist on the physical plane.

The worlds of desire and emotion are held in common in both kingdoms. They are inextricably joined – inextricably that is, until humans consciously take of this animal substance and from it fashion that being which is the fully-formed human being.

To humans it is uniquely given to harness the whole range of animal passions and to create from them an identity that is truly human. So do human beings form and shape their souls. Orthodoxy has rightly asserted that the substance of the soul is immortal. It is from this immortal substance that each must make and fashion that shape without which there is no enduring identity and no true individuality. These are the realities which are reflected in the physical relationship between the human and the animal.

The picture, then, that is beginning to emerge is that of a transformation taking place through the transmuting of energies of which the physical world is a reflection, a surrendering of lower forms of life to a higher, a movement upwards sustained and maintained by the conscious activity of human beings who are the instruments through which a divine purpose is being worked out.

It is thus given to humanity to be the means by which the energies of creation are taken up into the process of transformation, a process made possible by the death, resurrection and ascension of the glorified Christ.

There is another side of the picture at which we must also look. Where this process of transformation is not taking place, and where the human being fails to fulfil its destiny and assume its proper role within the created order, then another law is seen to be continuously in force. This is the law of eternal recurrence, from which humanity breaks free only in the finding of true identity.

Let us look again at the picture. Contained within each level of consciousness, rock, plant, animal and human, there operates an unbroken cycle. It is the perpetual recurrent wheel of life and death, an invariable and inexorable law of manifestation into form, a blossoming of life, followed by disintegration and decay. Again there is manifestation into form, and so the process is endlessly repeated. The gravitational pull of earth to earth, ashes to ashes and dust to dust can nowhere be halted or annulled. Mortality is writ large across all creation. The miracle of birth, the beauty of growth, blossoming and fruition must all be overtaken by death and destruction, and from corruption new forms arise to repeat the process.

Of this process St Paul's 'natural man' is an integral part. For the substance of such a human being there can only be the law of eternal recurrence, for this man is 'of the earth earthy'. In his physical form he belongs to the lower kingdoms of mineral and vegetable. To these his physical body must return and the substance offered to him by these kingdoms must be surrendered. The substance offered by the animal kingdom must also, if untransformed, be returned to source to remain part of what St Paul calls the animal body (1 Cor. 15). 'If', says St Paul, 'there is an animal body there is also a spiritual body.' Observe that the spiritual does not come first. The animal body comes first and then the spiritual. The first man is made of the dust of the earth, the second man is from heaven.

It is not only the pattern of this spiritual body within the individual that is being shaped. The Cosmic Being, Christ himself, of which all redeemed human beings are a part, is also being formed. The animal is surrendering itself to the spiritual, the transient to the eternal. Herein lies the fulfilment of the words 'that Christ may be all and in all'.

Another dimension of the process of transformation will open steadily to those who are learning to see. It is that of the angelic ministry. For within the lifting up of creation, a process which is both personal and universal, are divine agencies. They (unlike the elemental spirits) are operating to assist humanity in its ascending progress. These are the angels of God depicted in Jacob's dream (Gen. 28). They are seen ascending and descending upon a ladder set up between heaven and earth. Each of the kingdoms of creation has its angels, centres of consciousness capable of responding always and instantly to the magnetic pull of the divine source. Their function is to assist humanity in resisting the gravitational pull of the law of eternal recurrence. Present at every level of creation, they operate therefore within the total being of the human. They link the material and non-material worlds. Their function, in relation both to God and to humanity, is immediate. In every human response to the divine activity they are impulsively active. They make possible a true holy communion beween the human and the Divine or what may be called the flow of Holy Spirit. They are ever turned to God on our behalf. For as Jesus reminds us, the angels of the child and the child-like 'always behold the face of my Father who is in heaven' (Matt. 18.10).

As indicated, the responsibility for the lifting up of creation into meaning and purpose beyond the transitory belongs to the human being. Yet it is equally clear that this capability is not easily realized and released.

A powerful impetus towards planetary consciousness has been generated by the social and political upheavals of the past decade. But enthusiasm and dedication are not enough. Only when harnessed to those disciplines which cultivate discernment can they produce a creation spirituality which is something more than, on the one hand an evolutionary regression, or on the other ecological concern in religious dress.

13

People of the Way

Any realistic assessment of the significance of the New Age phenomenon must be made not only from the perspective of the established Christian Church but in relation to society as a whole; for by the same standards and criteria must the Churches themselves be judged.

Are the powerful influences which we have examined subversive, and conducive only to the destruction of society, as some would maintain, or are they in truth creative energies which, when harnessed to individuals and groups, and for a greater good, ensure the continuation and evolution of life on the planet? Again, are the new perceptions of reality, as some would assert, a serious threat to truth as perceived by the old religious institutions?

Here it is worth noting that these were the accusations directed against the Christian Church as it struggled to come to birth in the context of the Roman Empire, and against that new age heralded by the birth of Christ.

My own journey of discovery, begun in the early 1970s, leaves me at the beginning of the 1990s in no doubt that if giving space, place and cognizance to humanity's authentic potential, both intuitively and rationally, are hallmarks of the children of God, then the New Age no less than the Churches has given them birth, and is nurturing their growth.

If the releasing of that potential is evidenced by personal transformation and the cultivation of social and global responsibility, then New Age impulses no less than renewal movements within the Churches are providing impetus for this.

Do these impulses, having run their course, leave a residue of new cults? Certainly this appears to happen. No less is this the case when renewal movements within the ecclesiastical system give birth to House Churches, and House Churches establish themselves as new fundamentalist sects.

If, as is frequently asserted, the New Age arena is littered with groups which encourage and develop personality cults around teachers and gurus, the question must then be asked, does this not have its counterpart within those churches which substitute a Jesus personality cult for the New Testament experience of the indwelling Christ, and who like Mary Magdalene need to let Jesus go in order to acquire that greater vision to which he is the supreme pointer?

Psychic culs-de-sac abound in plenty, apocalyptic fallacies are devoured by the gullible, human nature is frequently romanticized and spurious experience often underlines the absence of that *gnosis* which the New Age at best exemplifies. All these are to be found. All such anomalies are equally apparent within those venerable structures to which we accord the title 'the Churches of God'. In neither case does such evidence of fallible human beings annul either the Spirit's presence and power or the working out of a divine plan and purpose embracing all.

'Who are you?' is the question I found myself repeatedly asking of my early encounters along the way. Perhaps the most satisfying answer was that given to me at the Salisbury Centre in Edinburgh by a woman doctor in her nineties. Dr Winifred Rushworth was greatly revered as the founder of one of the earliest holistic centres. 'We endeavour', she replied, 'to be the people of the way for the age in which we live and to be open to the movement of the spirit in our day.'

There is a belief held by certain Eastern mystics that every nation requires at all times at least twelve righteous men in its midst in order to prevent the collapse of society and to ensure

that the evolution of humanity continues. These twelve symbol-
ize the People of the Way.

The principle behind this belief may be found operating
throughout the Bible. In the book of Genesis we find Abraham
pleading with God to save the cities of Sodom and Gomorrah.
The pleading becomes a dialogue between the two and follows
a descending scale of numbers. At first he pleads, 'If there be
fifty righteous men, save the city.' He ends by imploring God,
'For the sake of ten.' When that number was not found the
cities were destroyed (Gen. 18).

Conversely Abraham became the father of the Jewish nation,
the spearhead of the divine activity, because he believed in
God. And because of his faithfulness God declared, 'I will bless
you and make you a blessing, and through you shall all the
nations of the earth be blessed.'

This vision of a God whose dealings with humanity are for
the sake of those who acknowledge his presence and power
expands throughout the history of the Old Testament. With
the rise of the later prophets the note of concern for the whole
earth is increasingly sounded. The twelve tribes are seen to be
custodians of that which is destined to become the inheritance
of the whole earth. With the prophecies of Isaiah all nations
are seen to go up to Jerusalem, that is to turn towards the
place where God is manifesting himself, and the whole earth
is filled with the glory of God.

In the New Testament the vision expands further and the
divine action is no longer seen as that of subduing the nations
and the negative elements within society. The emphasis shifts
to that of the redemption or raising of humanity. All are destined to become part of the great plan and purpose in which
the Deity and humanity are to come together. God is seen to
act in and through Jesus, and Jesus is seen to be acting; first
of all for the sake of the twelve. On the night before he was
put to death Jesus said, 'For their sake I set myself apart' (John
17.19).

'The twelve', both in the Old and in the New Testament

where it refers respectively to the tribes of Israel and to the chosen disciples, takes on a special significance. For in both instances it signifies the full human potential and every aspect of that potential. The totality of human possibility is there signified, and God's operation through the twelve signifies his dealing with the fullness of the human being.

Here it is important to distinguish two areas of divine activity. The primary activity is through those within whom true identity has been achieved, as in the case of the Apostles. It is there that we find conscious co-operation with the divine power, the exercise of wisdom. This is the means by which he draws the essence of all humanity towards himself, for his purposes extend to and embrace the whole human race.

'You are the salt of the earth and the leaven in the lump,' declared Jesus of the twelve (Matt. 5.13; 13.33). He also described them as 'little flock' to whom it is the Father's good pleasure 'to give the kingdom' (Luke 12.32). These are they who not only ensure the survival of the human race but who, as co-workers together with God, redeem it.

To approach it in another way – the twelve in every age constitute the spearhead of the human race in its evolutionary progress. They have discovered within themselves a potential which is able to lift them to a level of operation other than that of the animal. They share in the very energy of resurrection. Yet they do not despise nor reject either their own animality or that of others, for they know this is to be the stuff of what the kingdom of God is about. Every age, every culture and every generation needs its twelve if humanity is not to be submerged in the morass of animality which ever threatens to absorb the race.

The twelve, in the sense that we are using the word, describes those who rise above the conditioning which imprisons human beings within its limits of natural perception. They have discovered the way which releases them from these limitations and have become aware of, as it were, a divine strategy and plan for all creation.

Let us now look a little more closely at these men and women who bind themselves to a purpose which, in the words of Jesus, indicates that they are 'not of the world'.

These People of the Way may broadly speaking be seen to constitute three categories. The first of these is that of men and women of integrity. These are they whose lives conform to a very simple yet profound philosophy. They give themselves constantly and consistently to considerations other than self-interest. Against all natural inclination they move in the direction of the well-being of others, and because they have broken free of the powerful pull towards self-gratification they see clearly that which constitutes the highest well-being of another. Free from their own self-centredness, they are able to perceive with accuracy what constitutes this well-being.

Such people may or may not live by professions of faith. They may or may not operate within the Churches. They may not be 'religious', yet they always move as prompted by a deep inner assurance of purpose and direction. In their informed concern for others, informed that is by their intuition, they contribute powerfully to the raising of consciousness in those with whom they have to do, for their integrity has immediate impact upon others. They may be agnostic with regard to concepts of God, if indeed they have any! Yet in the essence of Godliness they hold a very powerful share. Many would fail in all tests of commitment to 'the true faith'. They are the people who are characterized by the term 'good will', and they are ever open to 'that Light which lighteth everyone'. These, though People of the Way, may be unaware of their great significance in the work of God, yet they consistently create space within which the transformation of humanity is effected. In this way they are truly transformers and pioneers. They negate nothing that is good; rather they cause goodness to blossom further as they recognize it wherever it may exist. They are amongst those of whom Jesus said 'of such is the kingdom of heaven'. They are powerful exorcists in society. Truly they abide in Christ.

Secondly there are men and women of faith. These consciously wrestle in their own lives and in others against the impossible odds and mountains which only faith can move. No adversity is able to quench their confidence in the fact of divine providence working within the human race. With the eye of faith they see that all things are possible, and with this confidence they order their lives and encourage others. Like the men and women of integrity, they create space within the human psyche for the work of God to take place. They see possibilities where none apparently exist, potentials both in people and situations which are hidden from natural understanding. Wherever they exist they give birth to a unity, a unity of the spirit. Such men and women are committed to the highest that they know. This highest may in their understanding have the shape of God or it may not. Nevertheless, because of their faithfulness, the light of Christ shines powerfully in their hearts and they are consistently extending the borders of the kingdom.

Thirdly there are the men and women of wisdom. Wise in their generations, these are the ones who share in the life of the Spirit and consciously co-operate with it. Amongst them are prophets and seers. These press forward beyond the limitations of their own understanding, with a clear expectancy of divine guidance. The wisdom of the Spirit then becomes theirs. To them it is given to recognize the people of integrity and those of faith, to draw them together, and to give place, space and cognizance to all that they do. Sharing in the divine wisdom, they are able to distinguish the false from the true, to look beneath the surface and to see meaning and purpose behind the multiplicity of contradictions within the lives of individuals and communities. Because their wisdom is not of this world, they will at times need to act contrary to expectations and against the norms of society, for their scale of values and the rule by which they measure are neither predictable nor according to secular or religious conventions. Their work is to absorb into themselves and transmute the unresolved or negative energies of the society in which they are set. This has a twofold significance: (a) the total disintegration of humanity is prevented and (b) a constant transmuting of human energies provides the substance of the new creation in Christ.

Such are the People of the Way. They have respect for outward form yet depend upon none. They themselves may move imperceptibly from one category to another as needs so require. Recognizing the great diversity of needs within their fellows, they revere all the great spiritual traditions and paths by which human beings seek union with the Source. Yet no static form, religious or secular, political or social, can trap them for they seek always to discover the truth of every situation and act accordingly. Rising above the confines of their own predilections they are able to move into a larger space where, through an understanding of the present, past and future are brought together and meaning is given to the whole. They are therefore powerful communicators of hope. They recognize one another not by identity of beliefs but rather by their common commitment to 'the truth as it is in Jesus'; experiential wisdom is the criterion by which they are to be judged. Walking in the Light of the World, they are the Christ-centred ones and members of his universal body. They are the saviours of the race.

The Omega Order

The Omega Order, founded in 1980, is a contemplative ecumenical order for men and women, based on the principles outlined in this book. The Order takes inspiration from the writings of two men, F.C. Happold and Teilhard de Chardin. Happold's proposition that a leap epoch is now taking place in human evolution resulting in a profound change of consciousness, and Teilhard's perception of a new Christ-consciousness, combine to give the Order its vision.

The Omega Order exists to extend the vision and is founded in the confidence that to those who will follow the path of 'experiential wisdom', that is the contemplative way, Christ is even now revealing a new and triumphant aspect of his former countenance.

The effects of this unveiling are apparent both within and beyond the ecclesiastical structures. A new understanding is permeating the whole range of human thought and perception. In the context of religion we begin to witness the change from devotionalism to interior awareness, and the scientific disciplines are opening to a new understanding of the nature of the universe.

The Order's activities are directed to encourage effective co-operation with these changes. The aims of the Order are:

1. To follow those spiritual disciplines which awaken the heart to the truth 'as it is in Jesus'.
2. To recognize Christ under all forms to the exclusion of none.

3. To encourage the new Christ-consciousness wherever it is found.
4. To work for co-operation with the evolving life of the planet.

The Mother House of the Order is Winford Manor, Winford, near Bristol, Avon BS18 8DW, to which all enquiries should be addressed.

Bibliography

William Arkle, *A Geography of Consciousness*, Spearman, 1974.

Roberto Assagioli, *Psychosynthesis*, Turnstone Books, 1965.

Robert Augros and George Stanciu, *The New Story of Science*, Gateway Edition, 1984.

Alice Bailey, *Esoteric Healing*, Lucis Press, 1953.

Alice Bailey, *The Reappearance of the Christ,* Lucis Press, 1948.

J. C. Bennett, *The Dramatic Universe*, Hodder & Stoughton, 1961.

Harvey Cox, *The Secular City*, Macmillan N.Y., 1965.

R. M. French (tr.) *The Way of a Pilgrim*, Triangle, 1986.

R. M. French (tr.) *The Pilgrim Continues His Way*, Triangle, 1986.

Helen Greaves, *Testimony of Light*, Latimer Trend, 1969.

G. I. Gurdjieff, *Beelzebub's Tales*, Routledge & Kegan Paul, 1950.

G. I. Gurdjieff, *In Search of the Miraculous*, Routledge & Kegan Paul, 1963.

G. I. Gurdjieff, *Life is Real Only When I Am*, Routledge & Kegan Paul, 1963.

G. I. Gurdjieff, *Meetings with Remarkable Men*, Routledge & Kegan Paul, 1963.

C. F. Happold, *Religious Faith and Twentieth Century Man*, Darton, Longman & Todd, 1980.

J. A. Robinson, *Honest to God*, SCM Press, 1963.

Kathleen Speeth, *The Gurdjieff Work*, Turnstone Books, 1976.

Peter Spink, *The End of an Age*, Omega Trust, 1983.

Rudolf Steiner, *An Outline of Occult Science*, Rudolf Steiner Press, 1962.

Rudolf Steiner, *Knowledge of Higher Worlds*, G. P. Putnam 1923.

P. Teilhard de Chardin, *The Phenomenon of Man*, Collins, 1959.

Leslie Weatherhead, *Wounded Spirits*, Hodder & Stoughton, 1962.

Simone Weil, *Waiting for God*, Fontana, 1959.